Israel's Development Cooperation with Africa, Asia, and Latin America

Shimeon Amir

foreword by
Abba Eban

The Praeger Special Studies program—
utilizing the most modern and efficient book
production techniques and a selective
worldwide distribution network—makes
available to the academic, government, and
business communities significant, timely
research in U.S. and international economic, social, and political development.

Israel's Development Cooperation with Africa, Asia, and Latin America

PRAEGER SPECIAL STUDIES IN INTERNATIONAL ECONOMICS AND DEVELOPMENT

Praeger Publishers New York Washington London

Library of Congress Cataloging in Publication Data

Amir, Shimeon.
    Israel's development cooperation with Africa,
Asia, and Latin America.

    (Praeger special studies in international
economics and development)
    Bibliography: p.
    1. Economic assistance, Israeli.   2. Technical
assistance, Israeli.   I. Title.
HC60.A55   338.91'172'405694   73-8170

PRAEGER PUBLISHERS
111 Fourth Avenue, New York, N.Y. 10003, U.S.A.
5, Cromwell Place, London SW7 2JL, England

Published in the United States of America in 1974
by Praeger Publishers, Inc.

Printed in the United States of America

After this book went into production, the Arab-Israeli conflict intensified and war broke out in October 1973. As a result, the political context of this study changed materially, especially with regard to African-Israeli relations. Most of the African nations have now broken diplomatic relations, and the Organization of African Unity, an amalgamation of 41 black and Arab African states, has issued a public denunciation of Israel.

In our opinion, these new developments in the African-Arab region do not alter the relevance nor the timeliness of this documentation and analysis of Israel's cooperation in the field of overseas economic development, particularly as this study is based on the personal experience of the author, one of the principals in these programs. On the contrary, it would appear more important than ever that this contemporary example of Israel's development cooperation with the nations of Africa, Asia, and Latin America be placed on the record for all to judge and evaluate in the context of recent events.

February 1974

An unusual dialogue on development has been maintained for 20 years between Israel and developing societies in Africa, Asia, the Mediterranean, and Latin America.

The Israeli experience in the transformation of its society, its land, and its economy carries many important lessons for other countries. Yet some aspects of Israeli history are unique and many of its experiences are not transferable. Consequently, one of the basic issues for students of Israel's cooperation programs is to locate the precise areas in which Israel's development history is of broader relevance.

In this book Shimeon Amir has described Israel's experience in development and the application of this experience to cooperation projects across the world. His general conclusion points to the universality of Israel's experience and its value for emulation and study elsewhere. He also discusses the ethical motives of Israel's development cooperation and its historical and traditional roots in Israel's Jewish heritage.

Israel's development cooperation has been constantly undergoing modifications as a result of the changing needs and interests of the receiving countries and of Israel's own possibilities. At every stage Israel has manifested its desire to participate in a worldwide enterprise to combat the misery and poverty that still afflict a great part of humanity.

Continuing efforts in this venture are for us both a moral imperative and a political necessity. They also bring a contribution of some value to a more harmonious vision of international relations.

Abba Eban
Minister for Foreign Affairs
of Israel

ACKNOWLEDGMENTS

The first chapters of the book were read by the late John Gedeist of Praeger Special Studies. His comments and suggestions, during our several meetings and through later exchanges of letters, were stimulating, inspiring, and encouraging. Upon his untimely death, Mrs. Pearl S. Sullivan offered to rewrite and to edit the book. Her assistance was invaluable, and I am deeply indebted to her for the time, work, and erudition that she put into this work.

I have received helpful comments on respective chapters, dealing with sectors of their responsibility, from Mrs. Mina Ben-Ziv and Messrs. Yizhak Abt, Gershon Fradkin, Yizhak Zarfati, and Akiva Eger. My colleagues in the Division for International Cooperation were most encouraging, and my thanks are due to Messrs. Shlomo Havilio, Azriel Harel, Shaul Ben-Haim, Moshe Aumann, and Gideon Tadmor for their assistance and comments. Messrs. Moshe Fuks, Israel Mei-Ami, and Sasson Sofer, junior staff members, rendered important assistance in research. Miss Reeva G. Gorr took great pains in typing and correcting the manuscript.

These are only a few of the many who made possible the preparation of this book, and to them all I have a debt of gratitude.

CONTENTS

Chapter

Since 1958, ten years after its rebirth, Israel has committed its experience and skill to projects of cooperation with other developing nations. Some 15,000 trainees from these nations have participated in its seminars, courses, and study tours of differing durations. Some 5,000 Israeli experts on official bilateral missions have served in these countries in addition to over 3,000 sent abroad by public or private corporations dealing mainly with developmental work. Another 1,000 Israelis have served on behalf of the United Nations and other international agencies.

In proportion to Israel's population (an estimated 3,200,000 in 1972) the number of Israelis involved in this cooperative, sharing effort is high, comparing most favorably with that of countries in the West. Israel's effort is also distinguished by the fact that it draws heavily on its own internal developmental techniques, operating from fact to theory and not vice versa, so that its program of international cooperation reflects genuinely mutual assistance between developing nations.

In this program of aid and counsel Israel does not follow the familiar practice of "concentration areas." Its projects and the experts that make them possible have been, and will continue to be, widely spread. In 1972, for example, approximately 700 experts on bilateral and multilateral missions served in some 60 countries; in the same year trainees in Israel came from about 80 countries.

There is widespread interest in the nation's activities in the field of technical assistance as such, quickened by the political situation in the area, by the belligerence of the Arab world, and by the continuing animosity toward Israel of Arab supporters everywhere. In the past few years factions of the revolutionary New Left have joined the critics of Israel's cooperation projects.

Unfortunately, too little has been written on the performance of Israel in the field of technical assistance—too little, that is, without reference to extraneous political considerations that sometimes are remotely relevant, frequently are imaginary, or, equally erroneously, are excessively laudatory, although they are not always founded on evidence that can be adequately documented. The source of this dearth of information regarding Israel's efforts in this field lies, ironically, in the character of Israel itself. If history has demonstrated that Israelis are excellent improvisors and very good performers, it has, unfortunately, also shown that they are very poor in reporting their own successes in this field!

I have been involved in Israel's activities in developmental cooperation for a number of years. I have served in several Latin American countries. Between 1962 and 1965, I was deputy director of the economic division in the Ministry for Foreign Affairs, responsible for matters of developing countries. In 1968 I was appointed Director of the Division for International Cooperation in the Ministry for Foreign Affairs, later supervising this division, among others, as assistant director general. Since 1970 I have lectured on related subjects at Tel Aviv University in the Department of Developing Countries.

This book is the result of extensive, animated discussion with hundreds of

Israelis and others in both developing and developed countries regarding problems of development, development cooperation, modernization in general, and Israel's own performance in particular. The views expressed here are entirely my own and do not necessarily represent the official views of the Government of Israel. They are perhaps best described as "reflections of a practitioner" and a man-on-the-scene. The book does not discuss general studies or general references. The few bibliographical notes refer only to those facts and opinions actually discussed.

I am frank to concede that the reflections and inferences I have drawn are those of a partisan. More than once in describing Israeli developmental advisors I have candidly appraised them as either good or fair. But I have maintained consistently that the great majority of them are dedicated to their mission and truly care for what they are doing. I maintain, too, that care for other nations facing developmental problems similar to those that beset Israel in its struggle for survival and deep involvement in the challenges facing sister nations everywhere are both characteristics of our people and irrefutable proof of their faith and optimism. I do not hesitate to suggest that this is perhaps the central quality of the family of Israel's technical cooperation.

I dedicate this book to the thousands of Israelis who were and are committed to development cooperation. It is my hope that, in its modest way, my book will encourage them to record their deeds, not for self-glorification but as object lessons reflecting the achievements, experiments, and failures that together constitute their work and serve as a guide to others yet to learn what they have learned in the field —beyond the study—with living, striving men and women.

It is my hope, too, that this book will express the solidarity and deep respect I feel for the great community of developers in emerging nations as well as in those more fortunate. The work recounted here is a testimony of admiration to national and international agencies everywhere in meeting the greatest challenge facing mankind in our time: eliminating the poverty now crippling much of the world and bridging the increasingly dangerous gaps between the haves and have-nots everywhere. We are all learning that poverty, disease, and unemployment are not preordained but are very tangible scourges that can be overcome and that their conquest requires of all men maximum effort in regional, national, and international cooperation.

In 1973 Israel celebrated its twenty-fifth anniversary as an independent, modern nation-state. The profound transformation it has experienced is itself vindication of its belief that the successful growth and development of a nation are possible, given the study, dedication, and cooperation of its men and women. Israel's experience and expertise, forged in trial and error, contains valuable insights for developing nations. This book tries to cite the more salient of these insights.

Israel's Development Cooperation with Africa, Asia, and Latin America

Almost since its rebirth Israel has been active in various fields of technical cooperation with developing countries. Many new nations in Asia and Africa emerged into independence during the same decade in which Israel reestablished her sovereignty. Prominent members of national movements, among them future leaders of new states, visited Israel and were impressed by her rapid, spirited growth. They noted not only the physical transformation of the country in its landscape and economy but also the human metamorphosis, the human transformation that occurred in this tiny state. The swift and successful assimilation of more than 1 million immigrants by a population that originally amounted to not more than half this number, immigrants from countries with totally different backgrounds, struck them, as it has struck others, as one of the most astonishing instances of "human engineering" of our times. In this wave of immigration Israel acquired a wealth of skills and techniques in various areas of "development in action." Among these acquired skills were rapid organization of health services, community development, educational and vocational training and readaptation, rural and urban housing projects, and the teaching of languages, skills, and programs clearly applicable to other parts of the world.

Basically, developing nations were interested in drawing upon the Israeli experience in programming their own development. It was only natural, then, that when Israel and the emerging nations established mutual relations, much interest was concentrated on the multifaceted problems of development and, more specifically, Israel's potential ability to assist other nations in their development. "Dialogue of development" became the central theme of bilateral relations beyond traditional diplomatic relations.

Despite obvious differences that made much of Israel's experience inapplicable elsewhere, a good deal of it could be adapted with great success in the newly formed states. Which elements were applicable and the optimum conditions of their success

1

became very important subjects in succeeding years in the "dialogue of development" that Israel maintained with its partners in development cooperation.

This dialogue had two basic characteristics, one originating in similarities of
approach, the other in differences. Most Israeli leaders and many in the new states
of Africa and Asia had a common ideological background and maintained intimate
ties with socialist movements in Great Britain and Western Europe. Some of them
were alumni of the same university, the London School of Economics—the alma
mater of, among others, the late Moshe Sharett, first foreign minister and later
prime minister of Israel, and David Hacohen, one of the founders of Solel Boneh,
the big building contracting firm, and of the Histadrut (the General Federation of
Labor), and the first Israeli ambassador to Burma. From the beginning, therefore,
these nations shared a core of working concepts that created a sound basis for
mutual trust and understanding.

On the other hand, the Israel labor movement, which determined the future
developments of the country to a great degree, adopted a highly pragmatic,
nondoctrinaire approach to major national issues. It became mandatory for its
leaders to translate abstract ideas into operational "Implementationism" (in Hebrew
bizuism), the concept that it is not enough to conceive a great scheme—one must
make it work—became a new species of doctrine, if you will.

This practical approach had its roots both in the ancient traditions of classical
Jewish culture and in the more modern era of Zionism and the Jewish national
movement. A prolonged internal dispute centered on the question of what should
precede what—cultural Zionism, which demanded education and spiritual preparation for nationhood as a precondition of other activities; political Zionism,
including diplomatic activity aimed at international recognition of the new Jewish
state; or what is called practical Zionism, immigration and the formation of
agricultural settlements and other economic units. This internal dispute was
resolved by compromise, a synthesis of all three forms of Zionism, coexisting and
advancing simultaneously.

"Implementationism" is a modern version of this syncretic approach. It
appealed greatly to leaders of other developing countries seeking advice on how to
find practical, quick solutions to problems facing them.

I can now say in retrospect that all of us considered national development to
be a much quicker and easier process than it proved to be. On the other hand, we
demonstrated, I believe, that Israel's approach—one of advancing practical, simple,
relatively limited, achievable projects—served developing nations more effectively
than nationwide, general, more grandiose schemes, and that no amount of meticu-
lous study or prolonged research can guarantee that such schemes will be effected
in fact as they are presented in elaborate reports.

Israeli cooperation projects developed reactively, in response to requests from
interested nations or from national independence movements. At first such requests
were studied on a case-by-case basis, and the required budget was improvised
according to the authority or persuasiveness of the concerned Israeli government
agency. No formal acts of either the Knesset or government decreed the institution
of programs of international cooperation. Indeed, only in early 1958 was a special
Division for International Cooperation established within the Ministry for Foreign
Affairs.

The earliest evidence of interest in Israel's developmental experience as a source of inspiration for other developing countries came from a Burmese delegation to the International Trade Union Congress at Belgrade in 1950. The Burmese delegation, visiting Israel on its way home, met with David Hacohen of Solel Boneh, who, as we have indicated, was Israel's first ambassador to Burma, where soon after Hacohen's arrival negotiations began leading to a wide range of cooperation on projects in agriculture, construction, navigation, and military assistance.

The second country to establish ties of technical cooperation with Israel was Ghana, which achieved its independence in 1957. Among the members of Israel's delegation to the celebration of Ghana's independence was, again, David Hacohen, who was naturally in a position to advise Ghana regarding possible projects of cooperation on the basis of his rich experience in Burma. Here, too, the future range of projects discussed was very diversified, embracing subjects as far-reaching as agriculture, water development, youth programs, and construction.

In 1958 Golda Meir, then minister for foreign affairs, made her first visit to Africa. Mrs. Meir was deeply moved by the enormous challenges and problems facing the young states of Africa after they achieved their independence. Upon her return, she made it clear to the Israeli government that she considered it Israel's duty, as well as the duty of other nations, to participate according to its capacity in efforts to close the growing gaps between developed countries and those in the process of development. Mrs. Meir expressed her belief that Israel could and should play a significant role in fighting these nations' grave problems of health, unemployment, education, housing, and malnutrition. She voiced her firm conviction that Israel, out of its own experience, was in a particularly useful position to offer these nations meaningful assistance, and that it was Israel's duty to offer the best possible aid to the neediest countries of Africa. In the same year the Division for International Cooperation started to function, and its activities became an integral part of Israel's relations with developing nations.

The original impetus behind Israel's programs of technical cooperation was both spontaneous and altruistic. Essentially, the same spirit still informs Israel's conduct in this vital sphere. The prime motive of Israel was defined by Mrs. Meir after her return: "They [the African states] are in great need and we must assist them." Her empathy and concern still govern Israel's conduct in this area of international relations.

Over the years Israel has also become involved in discussing with greater sophistication the motivation behind its programs of cooperation. One question is whether they have been recipient-oriented or donor-oriented,* to use the terminology introduced by E. M. Martin, chairman of the Development Assistance Committee of the Organization for Economic Cooperation and Development (OECD). As it turns out, it is most difficult to draw a line very firmly between the two types of development assistance projects. If Israel wishes to perform what she considers her duty, in Mrs. Meir's words, and help those in need of assistance

---

*Edwin M. Martin, "International Implications of Aid Programs," *Technical Assistance and Development, Proceedings of the Truman International Conference on Technical Assistance and Development*, Jerusalem: Harry S. Truman Research Institute, The Hebrew University, 1970, pp. 226-37.

according to her ability and to the needs and wishes of recipient countries, and thus create goodwill toward herself, can it be said that Israel's motivation is recipient-oriented or donor-oriented with any real justice? Is it perhaps both? Isn't any normal program of assistance between one nation and another a combination of altruistic and self-serving interests? We most certainly live in a world in which relatively steady and harmonious progress cannot be assured unless continuing efforts are made to eliminate developmental gaps between different strata of population throughout the world and to combat misery in its many forms. The tasks ahead are enormous—indeed, global in scope—and in embracing the wide range of human experience, they make any such discussion of motive and orientation both academic and irrelevant. A participant from Latin America at an international congress held in Israel, quoting a saying current in his country, put the matter well: *"El subdesarrollo es como Dios; está en todas partes."* ("Underdevelopment is like God; it is everywhere.") Our common desired objective can be put simply: to create conditions and machinery to transform the natural human impulses to combat misery in any of its manifestations into optimal development projects.

2

CRITERIA AND
GENERAL APPROACH

Much has been written about the need to define criteria of project identification and project evaluation. It is tempting to suggest that in this plethora of defining and redefining lies the crux of efficient development programming. For without doubt, if the development community were able to define and agree on the optimal criteria for identifying new programs and projects, sound priorities, and the means of their implementation, review, and evaluation, we would certainly witness considerable progress in developmental projects. As matters stand, we have yet to move adequately from the abstract to the concrete, to get out of the seminars and into the fields.

In spite of great efforts to improve methods of defining sound criteria of project identification, it is still difficult, at best, to posit generally accepted rules governing this area. Nor is this problem confined to underdeveloped countries. It is no less limiting in developed countries, as we can readily ascertain from the conclusions of the United Nations Conference on Human Environment, held at Stockholm in June 1972. As a result of this conference an entirely new complex of factors must be considered in the preparation of a new project, making the evaluation of criteria even more complex. It has been said that a good development project, properly conceived and executed, is one that solves more problems than it creates. It would appear that this dictum will become even more valid in an era more attuned to the dangers inherent in the ecological equilibrium.

Given the pragmatic nature of Israel's technical assistance and cooperation, only a few criteria governing them have been established for either identification or selection. They reflect a basic wish to achieve the objective of any viable development assistance program, to match as far as possible the needs of the recipient with the capabilities of the donor.

An almost generally accepted principle in any official development assistance program is delineation of the geographical scope of donor activities, usually defined

5

as a "concentration area." The basis for its definition can originate in geographical, historical, cultural, or even ideological affinity or interest.

Israel does not possess such a definition at this writing. Her activities, therefore, are worldwide. However, in those countries where there is a stronger mutual interest in various fields, there is also more activity in technical cooperation. This is particularly true in countries geographically close to Israel.

A very rough, very practical rule of thumb for the selection of projects, can, however, be adduced. Israel stands ready to consider any request for a technical cooperation project if three broad considerations are met: Is the project wanted? Is the project needed? Is the project's fulfillment within the scope of Israel's proven capabilities and potential?

The first two criteria are self-evident. Obviously only when a recipient country requests a project and the donor believes that this request will meet a real need can the third criterion even be examined. Equally obviously, consideration of the third criterion—indeed of all the criteria—is prolonged in the first phase, depending on the informal exchange of opinions and the joint examination of basic data, developmental plans, general objectives, and expectations, an exchange normally carried forward on the diplomatic level.

The possibility of meeting a request for assistance is determined, of course, by the availability of finances, manpower, and expertise. Israel concentrates on those sectors in which its expertise is well established or in which there appears to be a legitimate justification to direct the request to Israel rather than to other sources of aid and counsel.

This is only a schematic presentation of the complex work of project identification and selection. Many more elements are being considered, both implicitly and explicitly. Recently much more attention is being given to the question of whether the implementation of the project would have institutional impact and thus become of lasting importance.

Another issue widely discussed among technical assistance agencies in the world is the relative advantages of bilateral as opposed to multilateral assistance. Here once again, there are no fixed rules in Israel's policy and practice. There does exist, however, a continuing interest in coordinating new, ongoing projects with those of other agencies, both bilateral and multilateral.

We believe in the advantages of a multilateral approach of subcontracting parts of a wider project to a national cooperation agency vis-à-vis a more complete multilateral approach that would "eliminate" the nationality of the donor. A good example of an interagency approach is the project of vocational training in Thailand, which is based on joint action by the Thai government, the International Labour Organization, the United Nations Development Program, and the Israel Division of International Cooperation.

Several other joint, interagency projects have been going on. The agricultural projects in Laos and Cambodia have been executed successfully under the regional aegis of the Mekong Committee. The agreements with the Organization of American States and the Inter-American Development Bank on integrated rural development resulted in a number of successful projects in Central America, in the Caribbean area, and in South America.

The *sine qua non* of any kind of coordination with other agencies, of course, is the desire of the host country to act, as is full conformity with its development polices and plans in both the short and the long run. In this respect the developmental experience of different countries varies. Some nations have hesitated to opt for coordination with other agencies out of apprehension that this approach will unnecessarily prolong the preparations for and, in some cases, even the degree of scope and success of developmental plans. Some countries, on the other hand, have followed the accepted principles of current development strategy, favoring full coordination of development projects under United Nations aegis and the efficient coordination of all bilateral projects during the early stages of planning, preparation, and implementation.

When actual plans are being discussed for a technical cooperation project special emphasis is placed on establishing its viability in terms of local conditions. Unfortunately, donors too often tend to introduce and teach what they know and practice, not what the recipient needs and can usefully apply. Therefore a motto of Israel's experts is "Adapt rather than adopt." Israeli experts sent abroad and foreign observers and experts both in Israel and at home sometimes react in terms of "adopt" rather than "adapt"—and are at fault when a local Israeli institution, system, or technique captures their imagination.

An excellent example of this well-meaning but unwise reaction of "adopt" rather than "adapt" is the celebrated institution known as the *kibbutz*, which can be broadly defined as a collective farm or settlement governed by strict communal rules. Israelis have often had to warn foreign visitors of the enormous difficulties involved in transplanting the institution or concept of the *kibbutz* elsewhere and have suggested other forms of settlement more ideally suited to their visitors' needs and more adaptable to their milieu and traditions.

When Israel is approached with a request for advice regarding establishment of a new institution or system following an Israeli pattern, her intuitive reaction has always been to suggest first a thorough examination of the existing foreign establishment, an evaluation of the requested innovation in terms of its viability within the existing establishment, and, if needed and feasible, the introduction of simple variations and adjustments. The rationale behind this approach is as simple as it is obvious: Rather than suggest that visitors surmount *two* great challenges and changes—a new institution and new congeries of functions—it is presented as both cheaper and simpler to face only *one*. It is axiomatic that the chances of introducing successful change are much greater when changes are introduced experimentally and gradually than when they are arbitrarily imposed without deference to specific local needs.

Israel has sometimes received requests for advice on establishing a research institute, an apparently simple request. With research, however, it has been learned that the data requested could easily be found, stored, and processed elsewhere, thus obviating the need for a new institute. It is discovered quite often that those seeking Israel's aid and counsel already have the knowledge they are seeking but that the channels of dissemination are faulty. In other cases systems of research are isolated, their participants unaware that, given proper links with relevant sectors of the economy of their own country, the challenges they face can be fruitfully surmounted by them and their potential fulfilled. Clearly, cooperation between scientific, creative research and those involved in practical, productive sectors of national economies remains a great challenge, not to say an unnecessary internal impasse in many parts of the world.

"Institution building" *de novo* has been advocated by Israeli experts only in rare cases: those in which it has been firmly established that existing facilities cannot fulfill the necessary or desired function, when the function is essential, when a new institution does not cause needless antagonism, and, not least, when the requested or suggested change is relatively practical, simple, and inexpensive. Institutes for rural planners, in some cases established as separate entities and in others as integrated departments in existing educational establishments, serve as good examples.

In planning development projects Israel always recommends an *organic* approach. Ideally, a small experimental pilot project provides relevant data for the larger project. While this approach is slower in its earlier stages, it is both quicker and less expensive in the long run, eliminating hasty innovations on a large scale that might prove faulty, highly expensive, or unsuitable. Operating according to this more modest but financially wiser approach, Israel has often been criticized in negotiations with big development agencies for the small scale of her projects. Israel, in turn, has warned her critics against excessive and costly speed, stressing that enduring development and modernization are processes more difficult in practice than one would like to believe a priori. Israel has also stressed that pilot projects should be planned in terms of easy transformation into pioneer projects, with experience gained on a small scale widely disseminated.

The primary lesson learned after long and diversified experience, however, is that the major key to successful development anywhere is training and preparation of suitable manpower and personnel on different levels—skilled, semiskilled, technical, scientific, managerial, and, in the broadest sense, professional. No successful development project, small or large, can be achieved without a concentrated, well-conceived, and comprehensive effort to train manpower suited to real needs. Israel's technical cooperation, since its inception, has been concentrated on achieving these ends.

Developing nations have been interested not only in receiving professional Israeli advice in actual projects of development but also in the Israeli experience at large. Their interest has had its origin not only in similarities of challenges facing them as nations but also in empathy of both past and present conditions and of future aims and expectations. Israel, on its part, has empathized deeply with the developing countries because it is one of them, and because it believes that its own growth and development techniques and patterns hold worthwhile lessons for others.

The reasons for this empathy, this mutual awareness of shared problems and objectives between Israel and other developing nations, are complex and numerous. Israel achieved independence in 1948, within a decade or so of the time at which they did or within the span of their living memory. Israel, like them, has had to face tremendous problems of "human engineering," to develop a sense of fresh roots, a solidarity, a national identification among immigrants with differing, often conflicting, cultural backgrounds. Israel had to inspire her new citizens with a feeling of cultural unity, an identification with the aims of a fledgling nation-state. The fact that to a remarkable degree Israel has met this Herculean challenge head-on with success resulting in a widespread, even passionate dedication to both state and society that has in turn inspired her sister states throughout the world in their efforts to reach the same goals.

For example, the introduction of Hebrew as a living language of the home and of the streets, no longer the province of classical scholars, met with astonishing success. Children learned it in the schools from the earliest possible age. It was introduced in adult education. Intensive short or full-time courses of the *ulpan*, or conversation, variety quickened the interest and lives of Israel's new citizens. Hebrew soon served not only to facilitate the preparation of adult immigrants for their professions but, supremely, was a central factor in their assimilation and acculturation to their new environment.

Developing countries were impressed no less by the specific economic, social, and technological progress of Israel, immediately sensing the potential applicability to their own problems. The rapid economic development of Israel was from the beginning an inseparable concomitant of the nation's preoccupation with social progress. Israel never faced the dangerous situation that characterizes some developing countries—"growth without development." This is a potentially crucial problem of overall increase in national wealth subverted by increasing gaps of income among classes, the traditional situation of "the rich getting richer and the poor getting poorer." Even in the days before the establishment of the state, the Jewish population in Palestine struggled for a free, democratic society with a maximum of equality, a minimum of differences in standards of living among classes and between the rural and urban population. The striving for social justice and equality found ultimate expression in national ideology, formation of parties, and political organization. The predominance of labor-oriented ideology in party politics and in the very organization of the nation was a natural result of the widely shared belief of Israelis that without equality of opportunity, without social justice, no economic, social, or political program is either viable or ethically acceptable.

Because of its predominance in politics and its permanent, soul-searching preoccupation with ideological issues, the labor movement in Israel was split into several parties and factions from its earliest days. Two parties representing the majority joined after many years of negotiations and formed the Mapai Party in 1930. This was the forerunner of the Labor Party of Israel today. In spite of later splits and reunification, it achieved hegemony within the Jewish population of Palestine and in the Zionist movement as early as the 1930s. Since the establishment of the state it has played a preponderant role in the formation of Israel's governments, as well as other public bodies and institutions. It has received from 33 to 40 percent of the electorate's support in past elections for the Knesset. Together with a smaller sister party, Achdut Ha'Avoda, and a third labor party, Mapam— one of more doctrinaire character—it has enjoyed an absolute majority, or at least a decisive role, in the past Knessets.

Steady economic growth in Israel, accompanied by an increase of well-being among wide masses of the population was possible partly because of the pragmatic approach to national issues taken by Israeli leaders and Israeli society at large. There has been, and continues to be, a will to equate general aims with specific deeds. These deeds, not abstractions or generalities, constitute the facts of everyday life affecting the individual. Consequently, to define Israeli ideology is to identify concrete expressions of social justice, an ideal rooted in millennia of Jewish culture. If this ideal can be reduced to a few words, they would be these: an unceasing struggle against any odds for what has been called "the kingdom of heaven on earth," here and in our time.

Moved by this equation of idealism and empiricism, Israel has produced many institutions governing social organization, forms of settlement reflecting varying degrees of cooperation among its members and patterns of joint action among settlements. Especially creative has been the rural sector, perhaps because it represented a relative novelty in Jewish life, and certainly because it has acquired and has maintained a high rank in the social value system of Israel.

Leaders and intellectuals from developing countries have also been conscious of similarities between Israel's and their own problems in the sense of developing a national consciousness out of regional loyalties, introducing a unifying new language, and the transformation of skills. Of particular appeal to these foreign leaders have been Israel's changes in the sectors of agriculture and rural society in general, community action, and, especially, ways used to incorporate various elements of the population in the process of development. They have shared Israel's concern that social progress not lag behind economic growth. The practical, on-scene steps taken by Israel to attain these goals in tandem and the institutions established to implement them—the human technology of development—became focal areas of interest. Israel's planning of developmental processes, its organic and gradualist approach to solutions, working from viable pilot projects to more permanent structures to realize economic goals, all of which led to what might be termed an integrative approach or "closed cycles" of development in spatial dimension and in planning procedure, became subjects of intense study and application in developing countries.

The special interest in Israel's agriculture and rural structure is founded on a singular coincidence. Israel has succeeded in agricultural development to a remarkable degree, in some cases on a worldwide scale. In the developing countries in general the need to advance agriculture has been recognized as an absolute precondition of growth and progress. If in the 1960s some economists could still put forward the concept that developing countries might achieve successful overall development without modernizing their agricultural and rural structures, their position is now recognized as untenable. Clearly, predominantly agrarian societies cannot develop a modern, progressive economy without first modernizing their agricultural techniques and solving the attendant problems of rural unemployment or underemployment. In his address to the Economic and Social Council of the United Nations on September 28, 1971, Robert S. McNamara, president of the World Bank, declared: "To many in the countryside, it appears more attractive to migrate to the cities and wait there—even without work—in the hope of eventual employment, than to endure the poverty of underemployment in agriculture. So, solving the urban problem must be found mainly in the rural areas."

Another factor should be considered in this context: education. Israeli society has always concentrated on diverse modalities of youth education, both formal and informal. Various modalities of unconventional forms of education have also evoked marked interest in developing countries because the percentage of young people in these emerging nations is higher than in nations already developed.

Actual changes in Israeli society, diverse types of institutions created to meet real needs, innovations in rural society, community action, and special programs for youth—all of which represent different stages and forms of nation-building—have become the overriding focuses of Israel's cooperation programs with other developing nations.

AGRICULTURE AND RURAL SOCIETY

ISRAEL'S AGRICULTURE

Israel's assistance in agriculture and in the rural sector draws on diversified experience of more than a century. The very first agricultural school, in Mikveh, Israel, was established in 1870 by Karl Netter of the Alliance Israelite Universelle, a decade before the first wave of immigration to Israel. This was symbolic in many ways, but particularly in the information it brought to those concerned with the methodology of development:

1. Preparation of manpower and the development of human resources must precede actual fieldwork.

2. Agriculture is of prime importance and takes precedence over all other sectors.

3. Scientists and intellectuals must constantly be involved in both education and its pragmatic application to serve society at large, and must give their immediate attention to problem-oriented research projects.

The differing types of settlement and village, many of which are still extant, brought about a rich, diverse experience in agriculture. In addition to conventional villages, modeled on the European patterns and privately owned, hundreds of settlements with varying degrees of collective ownership and cooperative organization came into being. Variations even among those belonging to the same system or grouping arose, contributing to a gamut of organizational structures and thus enabling Israeli experts abroad to determine the most suitable modality of rural organization for any given locality by drawing upon their own experience.

Public ownership of the major part of agricultural land, introduced in the early 1900s, has been of great help in furthering development in agriculture. Speculative trade in agrarian land was thus eliminated, an important factor in controlling price fluctuation of agricultural products. A more important consideration was perhaps the social result—public ownership and control eliminated fragmentation and the formation of minifundia and, in turn, the buying up of large tracts of arable land and the creation of multifundia. Land tenure in agriculture, as it exists, permits steady development within a pluralistic system of ownership and organization, promoting a wide freedom of choice and constantly adapting to evolving needs.

The agricultural history of Israel, both conceptual and institutional, can be broadly divided into three periods:

1. *1880-1904*: formation of traditional villages, privately owned
2. *1904-48*: introduction of cooperatives and collectives, with concomitant development of concept, framework, structure, and modalities for their operation
3. *1948 to present*: large-scale settlement schemes, initiated by the state—in the first years after independence, massive absorption of new immigrants in agricultural settlements, mainly of the "moshav" type (smallholder villages), otherwise known as multipurpose agricultural cooperatives.

The first two periods contributed greatly to the prevailing scale of values—social, economic, and cultural. They largely represented the socialist concepts of the 19th century—utopian and humanistic—combined with traditional Jewish values divested of ritualistic aspects. Orthodox Marxism also contributed its part, but to a lesser extent. The Jewish labor-agricultural sector was imbued with considerable idealistic *élan*. An outstanding example was provided by one of the founders and teachers of the Labour Zionist Movement, Aharon David Gordon, who created a sort of layman's "religion of work," one concentrating on the moral duty of man to work—manually and with his whole being—particularly in agriculture. Agriculture, in addition to its moral, social, and humanitarian qualities, assumed national importance. It was proof of the return of the Jewish people not only to the home of their forefathers but also to the cultivation of its soil.

The third period saw the settling of tens of thousands of families in cooperative villages. These were mainly immigrants from North Africa, Asia, and Eastern Europe. The extraordinary, perhaps unique feature of this phenomenon was the transformation of urban populations into rural ones. This alone represents perhaps the most important source of inspiration in the conduct of Israel's cooperation with other developing countries. The old-timers had to invent new techniques for introducing modern rural institutions to large numbers of former city dwellers in a relatively short time. They were also faced with the need of introducing these immigrants to an entirely new milieu, helping them become accustomed to new surroundings, a new language, and an entirely new way of life.

From their observations during these periods, planners came to the conclusion that 70-80 inhabitants to a village was optimal, since that number was small enough to ensure social cohesion and large enough to warrant the rudimentary elements of organization and administration. A rural center was constructed in the midst of four or five such properly planned villages. This center provided facilities and services that single villages could not afford—a school, dispensary, store, bank, agricultural machinery center. Several rural clusters, each composed of a number of villages and a rural center, could become a region in need of a development town, with even more sophisticated services and industries for the advancement of the economy and the social structure of the area.

This organic planning approach leads to the formation of comprehensive regions (on a subnational level), integrating agriculture and industry, and economic, social, local, and national aspects of existence. With the advancement of rural productivity, the rural centers and the development towns generate employment for excess manpower released from agriculture by modernization. They constitute an important brake for a rural exodus by providing some of the amenities of city living in a rural area. Instead of transferring people from village to town to enable them to avail themselves of better employment and entertainment opportunities, every effort is being made to reverse the trend—to bring amenities and facilities offered by the cities to rural areas. Undoubtedly, if this is successful, it will result not only in economy but also in the diminishing of social tensions and their results in big urban centers.

Comprehensive planning, in Israel's experience, is the optimal combination of human resources and physical conditions to maintain an equitable balance of rural and urban populations. The factors creating productivity—such as land, water, proximity to a town, available manpower, and technological and scientific know-how—must all be taken into account in the various stages of microplanning (of individual farms) and macroplanning (of villages, rural subregions, and regions at large).[1]

Since many of these factors are in a constant state of flux, there is need for continuing feedback between planning and implementation. This requires allowance for all contingencies by planners, in order to permit future modification and change.

In recent years rural areas throughout Israel have undergone substantial transformation. Industry has been introduced in numerous villages and kibbutz settlements, and in 1972 it provided 50 percent of their total product. Evolution of services both in rural centers and in development towns offers employment opportunities for professionals, who ordinarily would have to seek their work in towns. A balance is struck between rural and urban populations, and this balance narrows the communications gap between them.

A close and permanent interrelationship between different elements of the population eases the adaptation of working patterns of the rural population to the demands of changing times. The immigrants who arrived after 1948 overwhelmingly preferred the family farm and naturally settled in moshav-type, smallholder villages. It was discovered that small-scale cultivation was not suitable for a number of crops —particularly those that cannot be grown economically on small, individual parcels. To take advantage of economy of scale and to make use of heavy machinery for cultivating and planes for spraying, a system of bloc cultivation was instituted. Adjoining individual farms are treated as a single bloc and cultivated as such by heavy machines, while functions that can be performed manually are carried out by the farmer-owners on their individual plots. In some cases the bloc is cultivated as an independent unit for a year, or perhaps a period of years, and the income divided among the smallholders.

For the new immigrants in some villages, two types of instructors were appointed. One group were experts in agriculture and imparted professional advice in agrarian techniques to newcomers; the other, a generalist cadre of "community development" officers, provided them with a knowledge of the laws and mores of the country in general, and with the organizational structure of the settlement movement and village in particular. The awareness that the process of modernization is complex, and that economic development must be accompanied by social and cultural development, was their guiding principle. The objective of transformation and modernization is the progress not only of agriculture but also of man—the farmer who carries it out—in his complex totality.

Training still plays a most important part in Israeli agriculture. The number of agricultural schools on the secondary level is increasing; in 1972 they had a student population of about 10,000. A recent innovation in professional schools is formal training for girls as agricultural clerks, thus offering girls a new, more sophisticated occupation. The Ministry of Agriculture maintains a very active and well-organized extension service that provides a wide range of constant, practical, day-to-day advisory services and conducts a series of professional courses of varying duration to meet the requirements of its clients.

One of the factors in the successful development of agriculture is the constant interchange of information and feedback between the producers, the extension services, and the scientific community. A considerable portion of government allocations for research, with the exception of security, is spent on agriculture. In 1970 the total budget of the National Council for Research and Development was $30 million, out of which almost a quarter was earmarked for agriculture. Apart from the introduction of new varieties through seed selection, the production of hybrid seeds, and the study of plant diseases, research is focused on the complex study of water. New systems of irrigation, such as drip irrigation, and new discoveries in plant physiology have made possible a considerable decrease in the allocation of water per unit of land without affecting the quality of the crops. Historical research in areas such as the Nabatean agriculture practiced some 2,000 years ago in the south indicates how runoff water can be used to expand areas of cultivation. Continual research is also being conducted, with a view to putting land to optimal use—for example, pasture land by dry herbage and animal husbandry. Last but not least are continuing efforts to find economical methods for the desalinization of sea and brackish water.

TRADITIONAL VILLAGES OF MINORITIES IN ISRAEL

Nearly all the phases and modalities of Israel's own experience in agriculture described so far have been put to use in cooperation projects abroad. One area of highest importance, however, has not been sufficiently studied or used—modernization of Israel's minorities: Moslems, Christians, Druses, and others. Some 100 such villages, situated within Israel's borders since 1948, have been living with their Jewish neighbors for a quarter of a century. Although they have been affected by the proximity of modern, advanced Jewish settlements, they have generally lagged behind in their own levels of economic production and social services. The government and the villagers themselves have been constantly preoccupied with ameliorating their conditions and bringing about a higher standard of living without disrupting the patterns of their traditional values.

A 1972 publication based on research conducted by an interdisciplinary team provides a methodology to establish elements of modernization and the relative position of each village, as well as suggestions for alternative developmental changes for each.[2] The members of the team and the project leaders combined the disciplines of rural planning, agricultural engineering, physical planning, regional planning, sociology, economics, and research. The team analyzed 94 villages inhabited by minorities and selected 50 for microstudy. This was the result of personal interviews with approximately 1,700 people chosen at random, each answering more than 200 questions.

The macrostudy came up with two independent measures of modern practice —the state of community services (or measure of consumption) and the potential for technologically advanced agriculture (measure of production). Nine typologies were established according to the dimensions of agricultural technology (irrigated agriculture and technology), community organization (attachment to the village, consumption patterns, communications with the world), and individual participation (departure from established family patterns, involvement with nationwide public institutions, and changes in occupation structure).

The anatomy of modernization of the traditional agricultural village contained in the study will certainly evoke in Israel itself conflicting opinions, as is the case with every new theory. There is little doubt, however, that even now some valid conclusions can be drawn regarding optimal modernization of minority villages and that in this process important lessons can be learned for facing such problems in developing countries.

In this context mention should be made of the tremendous progress of agriculture in Israeli-administered areas since the war of 1967. Agricultural production has increased from $50 million in 1967 to $95 million in 1971, a rise of 90 percent, while manpower employed in this field actually decreased from 45 percent to 34 percent. The pattern of extension services has not changed basically, nor have the Israeli agricultural advisors ever exceeded 10 to 20. This phenomenal growth has arisen from the apparent receptiveness of the local farmer to technological change, especially when he is confronted with innovations on a large scale, and his ability to see immediate proof of its success. An additional incentive to change has been the market for increased production, which has spurred efforts for further innovation.

PROJECTS ABROAD

In the actual planning of development projects in developing countries there has usually been a need to choose one of two alternatives: introduction of new concepts or systems in new areas where agriculture was not yet practiced, or the use of existing patterns of cultivation and concentration on changing only a few methods. If the first is followed, more spectacular results can be achieved, since the farmer is not hampered by old habits and procedures. Obviously this method is slower and more expensive, requires prolonged planning and preparation, and in the course of implementation may experience many unforeseen difficulties that result in delays and increased costs. Introducing innovations in an existing community, however, brings more rapid results because the innovative process is limited to a number of predetermined factors and there is less danger of unpredictable obstacles. The total effect of the second alternative is less impressive, however, and it is not always easy to introduce significant changes within an existing system or pattern.

The need to face this contingency was always present when Israeli experts were called upon to advise developing countries on whether to build new, well-planned, modern villages following a coherent regional pattern or to introduce elements of modernization in existing communities. Frequently a real choice did not exist and only one of the two alternatives was viable.

An official publication divides Israeli projects into two categories: those with predominantly socioeconomic objectives and those with predominantly agrotechnical objectives.[3] Among the specific goals of the first category are the channeling of agricultural development to areas of high economic potential and national benefit; the assistance in training of professional cadres; the encouragement of and active participation in institutions dealing with production, distribution, and consumption; the encouragement of change in individual habits; the facilitation of transition from extensive monoculture to specialized farming; and the amelioration of extension, credit, marketing, and other services for the development and settlement of new areas. The goals of the other category, predominantly agrotechnical objectives, concentrate on techniques of production by the individual and include communication of technical skills; introduction of modern agricultural methods, including the use of industrial inputs and introduction of new crops and improved varieties; and the introduction of agricultural implements and machinery wherever practicable.

The list of socioeconomic objectives is much more extensive than is the list of agrotechnical objectives and so, in fact, is the emphasis on projects in each category. In addition, even projects that have as their primary objective the increase of the farmer's agrotechnical skills cannot be executed successfully without at the same time developing and strengthening pertinent economic and social institutions and bringing about significant organizational changes.

In fine, the agricultural projects receiving Israeli advice, initiated and carried out during the period 1963-68, are classified by this publication into four basic types:[4]

1. Specialized projects
2. Establishment of agricultural farms
   a. Demonstration farms
   b. Training centers
   c. Observation and experimental farms
   d. Experimental and seed production farms
3. Organization of specific rural institutions
4. Comprehensive regional rural development projects.

Specialized Projects

Of the 43 specialized projects, 19 are located in Africa, 7 in Asia, and 17 in Latin America. Of these, 4 are classified as surveys and 9 are described as "project completed." Most of the projects involve a single crop or branch of agriculture such as cotton, poultry, or afforestation. A few refer to a single institution, such as an agricultural school or an agricultural marketing system. All are by definition single-purpose projects with a single objective and do not involve major changes outside the scope of the project.

Of particular note is the pest-control project in El Salvador. It was initiated after a severe attack by cotton pests in 1965-66 that reduced the area under cultivation by about 75 percent and resulted in tremendous economic loss to both the country and its farmers, as well as depriving innumerable laborers of their chief source of income.

A small Israeli team introduced the method of efficacious field inspection and a reduction in the number of sprayings. Excessive anticipatory spraying had resulted in unnecessary expenditure and was actually harmful to the crops and to the surrounding area because it disrupted the biological balance. After experimentation in a small area and the launching of a suitable extension program for field inspectors and pest-control technicians, the operation was expanded and successfully introduced into most of the afflicted area. Substantial reductions in outlay per unit area, made possible by efficient use of pest-control techniques, helped to restore cotton-growing to its former position as an important cash crop and as a source of livelihood for the great number of cotton pickers. After the success of the El Salvador program, many countries in Central America manifested interest in similar projects.

The improvement of cotton cultivation was an important element in a large-scale project of agricultural development in the Adana region of Turkey. An Israeli consulting company was involved in this project, financed largely by the World Bank.* After the coordination and active interest of the various national agencies involved in the development of the area had been assured, a program was agreed upon and established and a coordinating interdepartmental committee appointed. The next step was to organize the extension work necessary to carry out the plan. Instructors were selected from functionaries performing other duties who were then trained to work as extension officers with farmers and to concentrate on the major aspects of irrigation, pest control, and the use of fertilizers. The average yield of cotton rose from 1.4 tons per hectare (2.471 acres) to 2.5 tons per hectare during the first few years, and up to 3 tons per hectare later on.

The Establishment of Agricultural Farms

The establishment of agricultural farms encompasses 29 farms, 18 in Africa—including 10 youth farms—5 in Asia, and 6 in Latin America. Of these three are listed as being in stage of planning. Their common denominator is the small size of the farms that serve a variety of purposes, such as experimentation center, pilot project, or demonstration unit, with the potential for substantial multiplication if they prove successful. Too often in recent development history large-scale projects

---

*This project is not included in the above list since it falls under projects carried out by Israeli companies, described later.

have been undertaken and substantial outlays have been wasted when they did not prove successful.

Small-scale projects are useful not only for experimental use of new crops, new inputs, and new techniques but also for demonstration purposes. Until the farmer is convinced of the usefulness of innovations and is ready to accept them, it is wasteful to prepare for their introduction, even when they present no special problems in the purely agrotechnical context. The Tadzewu cattle ranch in Ghana and the Boyaca project in Colombia serve as excellent examples of demonstration projects. They show how total farm production can be improved usefully through modern agricultural or animal husbandry techniques and how they can be integrated in the existing farm system.

These types of farms, however, can produce the expected results only when they possess ample provisions for the training of local personnel at various levels and in suitable methods. Visits to farms, far and near, must be facilitated so that these farms can serve as demonstrations in fact as well as in theory. Transportation and arrangements for these visits are conducted by the extension service, which through its wide publicity efforts kindles the farmers' desire to see the projects.

Training farms for prospective farmers differ considerably. A number were established as an integral part of the youth programs; these will be dealt with later. An unusual type of training farm is the *"finca-escuela,"* which originated in Venezuela and was later adopted in the Dominican Republic. In each case a larger-scale farm was set aside in a major development project. Prospective settlers started working on the farms as laborers with a fixed wage and a share of the profits. Their share of the profits was held in escrow and distributed after permanent settlement. The farms were managed by the respective agrarian institutions. The farmers worked for two seasons, acquired practical knowledge of modern farming and of local conditions, and made obligatory savings. They were then settled in a planned village as individual farmers. This method was found viable and was later practiced, with variations, in Africa and Asia. In some cases, as in Thailand, the farm, after settlement by the farmhands, served as an observation, experimentation, and demonstration unit for the entire region.

The "finca-escuela" is an adaptation of the administered farm system applied in Israel during 1955-58. It enabled prospective, inexperienced settlers to get practical knowledge of agriculture and to postpone final parceling of land to a later stage. This system is particularly advantageous in countries with the problem of which settlement pattern to adopt. Planning for flexibility and possible change was introduced in several Latin American cases, known as "Plan Quizás" (Plan Maybe).

Again, it should be stressed that the typology and classification of farms is an ex post facto rationalization. Many of them served functions beyond those called for in their original plan, even if these functions had no connection with their chief purpose. This also proves that development is a complex process, and in order to be successful, should be as multifaceted as possible.

Petrolandia

Although the seed production farm is listed as a farm, it really comes within the category of specialized projects. The Petrolandia project, in Brazil, was part of a comprehensive regional program planned to increase considerably the very low income of the farmers in the poorest region of northeast Brazil. Its object was to raise yields through the use of improved seed production and to establish a number of modern farms for intensive seed production as well as to establish a training demonstration center for seed-production and plant-breeding personnel. It was also planned to become the principal farm for production of stock seed and genetic improvement for a wide region.

The project was implemented successfully. During five years of service by Israeli experts (1963-68), a farm for hybrid maize was initiated, planned, and built up almost to the target of 400 hectares. Another 400 hectares was prepared to cover an envisaged 800-hectare area. A Brazilian team of agronomists, scientists, and technicians was organized. A suitable unit to cope with increased production and marketing was established. After the phasing out of Israeli experts, in accordance with the original plan, local institutions executed the expansion of the program with complete success. One of the chief socioeconomic objectives presenting a real challenge envisaged the transfer of the operation of seed production from the status of a publicly owned and centrally managed entity to private commercial firms controlled by the farmers themselves.

A later study conducted by the Rehovot Settlement Study Centre, which specializes in problems requiring an interdisciplinary approach, presents a double evaluation: one of the project itself and another of Israel's participation in it.[5] It is a penetrating and critical study, sparing no one even on the basis of minor evidence. The chief criticism of the economics of the project is the gap between expected and actual farm yields. One of its most important conclusions is that the targets originally set were too high, on the basis of overoptimistic assumptions. According to the study the greatest achievement of the project was the successful training of personnel who could accept complete responsibility for every aspect of the project and expand it without foreign assistance. The project also succeeded in highlighting the importance of proper seed preparation in relevant institutions as an element in the modernization of agriculture and consequently it was decided to create seed farms in other parts of the country. This in itself is the main proof of its success because it demonstrates the multiplier effect of the project.

The authors of the Rehovot study rate the Israeli team's performance as generally satisfactory but lacking in sufficient understanding of local habits and ways of thinking. Israeli experts were pressing for the swift achievement of results, unaware that realization of expected changes depended to a great extent on evolution in organizational structure outside the project—and that cannot be achieved with speed. This criticism was also leveled by local functionaries directly connected with the project. Officials of higher rank were most appreciative of Israeli expertise and were not aware of the criticism leveled by their subordinates. Perhaps the greatest compliment was voiced by a renowned economist, Dr. Roberto de Oliveira Campos: "You [Israeli experts] demonstrate faith and that is the strength of the matter. There are results because you demonstrate faith in the Brazilian man. "[6]

The Rehovot authors state that during their examination of the project, a decision to transfer the farm from public to private ownership and operation had not yet been made. That an official publication, based on data only one or two years older than the study, mentions this among other feasible plans for the imminent future is additional proof of Israel's faith in man—an expression of optimism despite an insufficient appraisal of difficulties.[7]

Organization of Rural Institutions

Supervised Credit

Our discussion of specialized projects and different types of farms has demonstrated the extent to which Israel's assistance programs are involved in noneconomic factors of development. This tendency is even more marked in two remaining, more complex categories of agricultural assistance—organization of rural economic institutions and projects in comprehensive rural development.

Israeli projects of assistance in the organization and development of economic institutions during the period 1963-68 were carried out in three African, two Asian, and four Latin American countries. In the period 1968-72 similar projects in Latin America doubled in number.

The most urgent requests for Israeli expertise have been presented in the areas of rural credit, marketing, and extension methods. Quite often requests have combined elements of one or all of these functions in a single project. The supervised credit method, for example, is a synthesis of all three. It envisages a clearing system of accounts whereby a farmer receives bank credit in the form of agricultural inputs while his production is assisted and approved by an agricultural instructor; the farmer pays for his credits with marketing proceeds in a centralized system under the aegis of a village committee. At the end of the agricultural season, the bank pays the balance due the farmer in cash.

The supervised credit method ensures more efficient marketing and less costly acquisition of inputs. It reinforces the authority and leadership of the village committee and eases the process of modernization. If there is satisfactory progress in its application in the purely agroeconomic field, it can be extended to additional services needed by the farmer, such as health and educational assistance.

This system was introduced in 1964 as a pilot project in a Venezuelan village to finance a single crop. Proved completely successful there, it was expanded considerably in a short time. By 1968 the project was extended to serve farmers in 134 villages in 13 regions.[8] Farmers' income increased markedly—on an average of threefold—and systems of improved cultivation, embodying aspects of planning, extension, and marketing, were widely introduced.

A later publication contained details of the supervised credit system for 1970 and plans for 1971.[9] The number of families included in the system approached 20,000, embracing some 300 rural associations; the extension of credit planned for them exceeded 100 million *bolivars* ($20 million). Seven years earlier the system had covered only 77 families receiving a credit of 180,000 *bolivars* ($36,000) for a single crop. Until the new system was introduced, the rate of repayment varied from 20 percent to 40 percent of the credits. With the new system it rapidly increased to 70 or 80 percent and even higher.

In evaluating the overall results of this system Venezuelan officials cited a number of key issues apart from those already mentioned. They referred, for example, to marked increases in production and income, modernization of agriculture, and notable improvement in community services. The system's success enabled Venezuela to get large-scale development loans from the Inter-American Development Bank more easily. It also served as a source of inspiration in the introduction of the system in other countries, not only in Latin America but also in Asia. Not the least important factor in this development has been the human factor, well expressed by Wenscallo Mantilla, former president of the Instituto Agrario Nacional (*IAN, National Agrarian Institute*). In Mantilla's view farmers' success within the system of supervised credit and resulting increased yields were instrumental in "the strengthening of their self-assurance and their pride, having discovered that they [were] able to produce more."[10]

Criticism regarding introduction of the system was concerned mainly with the eagerncss of the initiators of the plan and of foreign experts to achieve swift results. As a result the agricultural instructor occasionally assumed the major burden of work preparatory to the credit system without permitting sufficient involvement of local community leaders in the process. Zeal, to put it briefly, occasionally slowed down the development of human resources.

Venezuela

Technical cooperation in Venezuela was significant in more than one way. It was in that nation that cooperative programs in Latin America got their start. These programs were expanded to other countries on a bilateral basis. Very successful and valuable ventures were developed jointly with the Latin American system through the Organization of American States (OAS) and the Inter-American Development Bank.

In its initial years—1963-67—Israeli activity in Venezuela was diversified. At the same time it was characterized by unity of purpose and concentration of effort, permitting the small team of Israeli experts to operate more efficiently by enabling them to share important conceptual support, thus creating an Israeli-Venezuelan version of "development doctrine."

Israel's participation in the agricultural development of Venezuela had its genesis in the enactment of Venezuela's Law of Agrarian Reform in 1960. One of the law's direct results was the formation of the IAN, the objective of which was to fulfill the law's social function, that is, to assure the farmer a decent income. If they were to achieve their objectives, the legislators realized, farmers had to be given this assurance of greater financial gain through an efficient extension service and a satisfactory credit organization. They were acutely aware that too often failures in agrarian reform were caused by the farmers' being offered only land, without the supporting services of modern know-how, organization, investment, and advances in credit facilities. They were also aware that as a result of these factors, the economic outcome of agrarian reform efforts was frequently negative. Instead of producing in bigger units utilizing economy of scale—centrally and efficiently administered, well-equipped, and open to technological innovation—the program of agrarian reform often resulted only in distribution of land into small units, without either central services or the advantages of economy of scale.

Aware of these dangers and resolved that the Law of Agrarian Reform would raise the farmer's standard of living, the Venezuelan government made sustained efforts from the inception of its new program to assure the farmer of these essential ancillary services. The newly created IAN soon established working relations with other government agencies, such as "Cordiplan," responsible for national planning; the Ministry of Agriculture; the Agricultural Bank; the Ministry for Public Works (in charge, among other assignments, of irrigation); the Ministry of Health (responsible for rural housing); and Programa Integral del Desarollo Agrícola (PRIDA, Integrated Program of Agricultural Development), charged with the coordination of agricultural projects in no fewer than 500 villages.

In 1961 the Venezuelan Ministry of Agriculture asked its Israeli counterpart to send a senior official for a number of weeks to conduct consultations on problems of agricultural development. This visit took place. In 1962, following the casual visit of another Israeli agricultural expert, discussions were initiated regarding the possibility of an Israeli team of experts coming to Venezuela for a longer stay to advise on integral planning of a rural region. The Israeli team arrived in 1963, its main objective to advise on integral planning of a new region in Las Majaguas, in the state of Portuguesa, in central Venezuela.

The Israeli plan advised detailed objectives of integrated development of the region, covering physical, economic, social, and cultural areas and aiming both at a higher income for the farmer and his successful assimilation into regional and national cycles of activity. With the assistance of Israeli experts following patterns proven viable in their own land, plans were made for the settlement of 2,000 agricultural families and a comparable number of families employed in industry and services. The farmers were to be settled in villages of 80 to 100 inhabitants. Provisions were made for rural centers, infrastructure feeder roads, and an irrigation system based on the utilization of the Las Majaguas lake.

In the subsequent implementation of this project the Israeli team played a reduced role. Although a small part of the Las Majaguas plan was actually implemented, its execution had a decisive effect on the development of agricultural and rural society. The system of supervised credit described above was introduced here. Not less important, and perhaps of an even greater multiplying effect, was another rural institution, evolved during the operation of the Las Majaguas project: the training and research institute Fundación para Capacitación y Investigación Aplicada de la Reforma Agraria (CIARA, Foundation for Training and Applied Research in Agrarian Reform).

When programming the implementation of the Las Majaguas project, Israeli experts suggested the institution of a course of study for comprehensive planners. This suggestion was eagerly accepted; and in 1963 the first course in comprehensive planning was held for graduates in the fields of agriculture, economics, architecture, and sociology. In 1964 another course, this time for technicians, was instituted in supervised credit. At the same time discussions were carried on regarding the possibility, need, and usefulness of a permanent institute to train manpower essential to the successful implementation of agrarian reform. In 1966 such an institute—CIARA—was formally inaugurated. Its objectives as stated by its founders, were the training of personnel for agricultural development, the preparation of projects for settlements, the investigation and evaluation of projects, and putative advisory and supporting services for the implementation of projects both at the center and in the field.

The principal function of the institute was obviously training. The scope of the subjects it offered and the rich professional variety of its participants have demonstrated both the important functions that CIARA fulfills and the problem-oriented nature of its programming. During the period 1963-69 almost 1,200 participants took courses in comprehensive planning, physical planning, supervised credit, farm management, agricultural techniques, marketing, hydrogeology, rural community organization, training methodology, and other subjects. Most participants were agrarian and agricultural technicians. Others included village leaders, economists, sociologists, and engineers.

Sufficient data to determine the extent of CIARA's success in fulfilling its objectives, beyond training as such, have not thus far been available. While it is certain that CIARA has participated in the preparation of important regional projects, it can be said that the most important cumulative result of its activity has been a general and fundamental change of attitude toward agricultural planning. According to Wenscallo Mantilla, president of IAN since CIARA was established, rational planning in agriculture was started on the basis of collection of data, careful preparation of projects, and the comprehensive approach to planning.

The numerous particpants in CIARA courses who were specialists at institutions involved in agrarian reform acquired a common language in rural development. Perhaps this was the major contribution of Israeli experts in Venezuela. The director of the Water Department in the Ministry of Public Works, a graduate of a course in comprehensive planning, stated that the concepts he acquired there were most useful and that he tried to apply them in the planning and development of villages.[11] Dr. Mantilla believes that the Israeli approach, as accepted and presented by CIARA, brought about productive cooperation of professionals and fieldworkers in actual development work. He was especially impressed by the fact that the Israelis never tried to present their concepts in a rigid, doctrinaire spirit but were consistently willing to discuss and reevaluate them and remained open to new ideas. "They succeeded in becoming genuine partners," he stated, "and at the same time eager and able to arouse local enthusiasm for programs."[12]

CIARA also succeeded in inculcating its students with the need to consider development as an integrated process and, from the outset, to concern themselves with community needs. As a result they learned the absolute necessity of ensuring coordination of the work of all ministries and institutions involved or performing related functions. One consequence of this approach is that no staff member involved in a given project would even consider a ministry's initialing of a new irrigation system, for example, as sufficient or conclusive, without planning and coordination with IAN and other relevant ministries.

Among the participants in CIARA courses in Venezuela were a great many students from other Latin American nations. Many of these countries, aware of the Venezuelan successes, asked specifically for Israeli assistance "according to the Venezuelan model." The chief of the institute for agrarian reform in Colombia, for example, requested that a course in supervised credit and physical planning patterned after the program of CIARA be given in his country. In addition, CIARA was instrumental in conducting similar courses in almost all of the countries of Central America. CIARA's performance has been held in high esteem in the Inter-American Development Bank. Approval of credits has been facilitated through provisions to train manpower for projects using the CIARA organization.

The first years of developmental cooperation in Venezuela can be characterized in three salient ways:

1.   Flexible adaptation of programs to predominant local needs. The decision to concentrate the efforts of the Israeli team on building up a training institute was a later development not envisaged in the planning stage.

2.   Stress on a comprehensive and integrative approach to development. All three projects—Las Majaguas, CIARA, and supervised credit—demonstrated the need to regard economic and social aspects of development as a single entity and to secure the coordinated efforts of all relevant agencies and institutions from the very beginning. Emphasis was also placed on the continuing character of development. The farmer had to be assured of essential supportive services for a long time. While CIARA was originally envisaged as an institution that, in addition to its training function, should advise and support the farmer for a number of reasons, its actual performance did not evolve according to the plan.

3.   The multiplier effect, a goal broadly discussed in development projects but not sufficiently clear in its concrete expression, was seldom satisfactorily accomplished. The establishment of CIARA and its manifest impact, both inside and outside Venezuela, however, can be considered as a practical example of successful achievement of the multiplier effect. CIARA succeeded in imparting knowledge and achieved practical changes in actual development within the relevant sectors.

An institution like CIARA can achieve even greater impact by applying its concepts to other sectors. It is only natural, for instance, to expect that graduates of CIARA would be inclined to transfer concepts of the unified social and economic approach to other fields under their direction. This is an aspect of the multiplier effect that can be achieved chiefly by establishing a permanent institution combining teaching, research, publication, and fieldwork and thus, over a period of time, developing elements of a school of thought or "doctrine" to be applied in a variety of relevant sectors.

Brazil

The ramifications of Venezuela's experience were demonstrated in various forms in numerous places. In Brazil the first course in comprehensive regional planning was taught from October 1971 to April 1972 at Fortaleza and was inspired by, among other factors, the successful example of CIARA.

Israel has been active in technical cooperation in agriculture and in comprehensive planning in Brazil under an agreement signed at Recife between the government of Brazil and the government of Israel in 1962. A mission of Israeli experts arrived in Brazil shortly thereafter and, under the supervision of SUDENE, the Development Authority of the Northeast, began work on a number of projects, one of them being Petrolandia. Others included assistance in planning and establishing new settlements, diversification of traditional crops, and utilization of dams. In 1967 a specific agreement was signed between the two governments for the development of a regional settlement project in the state of Piauí, also located in Brazil's Northeast.

Brazil's Northeast has been the preoccupation of its federal government for a long time. It is the home of 20-25 percent of Brazil's population, but its standard of living is considerably lower than in other parts of the country. Because the majority of its population is employed in agriculture, its programs for development must start with agriculture and rural society. It is easy to see why Brazil was and continues to be interested in the Israeli experience.

In addition to official agreements and formal projects of cooperation, including missions of Israeli experts to Brazil and study tours by Brazilians in Israel, several independent Israeli commercial firms were commissioned to carry out studies and execute projects related to similar planning. Simultaneously important and fruitful contacts were developed with various institutions in the Northeast, among them several departments of the University of Fortaleza and the Central Development Bank of the Northeast.

The very idea of conducting a course for comprehensive rural planning in the Northeast arose in an organic way as a result of the presence of Israeli experts in the area and visits of numerous Brazilians to Israel. It was felt that Israeli experience contained elements important to Brazil.

The course was initiated by the Banco do Nordeste do Brasil and the Federal University of Ceará for Brazil, and by the Settlement Study Centre of Rehovot for Israel. The Israeli institution, established in 1962, was sponsored by the Settlement Department of the Jewish Agency and the Ministries of Agriculture, Interior, Labour, Housing, and Foreign Affairs to serve as an independent study and research institute to conduct interdisciplinary applied studies in economic, agrarian, and sociological problems of both rural and urban communities, as well as for comprehensive rural planning. It emphasizes the integrated approach, interdisciplinary teams, and need for studies conducted jointly by scientists and by people with field experience. These studies may be commissioned by the sponsoring bodies or by other interested organizations in Israel or elsewhere. Usually the requests are problem-oriented and require preparation of actual studies. These studies offer alternative solutions to problems such as modernization of traditional villages, rural-urban migration, intervillage cooperation in agricultural production services, and patterns of employment in second and third generations in cooperative settlements.

The presence of the Ministry for Foreign Affairs among the sponsors and on the Board of Directors of the Centre manifests the interest of the sponsors in achieving feedback between Israel and the developing countries on related problems. The utmost expression of this interest is the one-year postgraduate course in comprehensive regional development. The first course was offered in 1965, the second in 1969. It has been continued regularly since that time. In 1973 the Centre inaugurated the first complete, parallel course in Spanish for the Latin American countries.

The Study Centre has been recognized by the United Nations as one of three institutions in the world for the teaching of comprehensive regional development. Members of the Centre have been active on a global scale, advising on problems of regional development. A recent example is the course on development planning organized by the Mekong Committee of the U.N. Economic Commission for Asia and the Far East.

The course set up at Fortaleza, Brazil, in 1971 drew on Israel's own experience and on the experience of Israeli experts in Latin America, particularly where projects of comprehensive regional planning were being carried out. The course was prepared by the Settlement Study Centre in a joint effort with the International Agricultural Cooperation Centre of the Ministry of Agriculture, the largest official Israeli agency for assistance projects. It was originally intended to achieve permanent communication between ongoing projects involving Israel's participation in Brazil and the course. In practice, however, difficulties arose and there was little, if any, rapport between teachers of the course and experts in the field; but there was constant utilization of past experience. Israeli lecturers were for the most part experts with actual field experience in Latin America. In addition, participants visited an operating project with Israeli participation and otherwise studied projects in Latin America.

The participants in the course were mainly agronomists. Other professionals included economists, managers, and engineers. Almost one-third of the teaching hours were dedicated to a practical exercise in comprehensive planning. This exercise was referred to as the planning of Acaraú Valley in the state of Ceará, covering an area of some 20,000 square kilometers (7,780 square miles) and located 260 kilometers (161 miles) from Fortaleza. The area has a large lake that could become a suitable source of both irrigation and the development of about 10,000 hectares.

The Brazilians taught basic subjects—economics, geography, sociology, agriculture—with special emphasis on the area of future practice, thereby contributing to intellectual and emotional identification with the assignment. The Israelis concentrated on the concrete aspects of their expertise in human technology in development. Their subjects included regional development, physical planning, agricultural planning, planning of production, and economic analysis of projects.

The students prepared preliminary surveys before the final exercise, which lasted only six weeks. Studies, conducted by interdisciplinary teams, included surveys of soil in the area selected for settlement, sociological factors, random production calculations for selected crops, marketing, and water resources.

The final exercise comprised four stages:

1. Data collection and discussion of existing surveys

2. Macroprojection of the whole region and definition of development goals under existing limitations; definition of relative stages of development in agriculture, industry, and services; particular examination of concrete possibilities applicable to agriculture in terms of the conclusions of the macroprojection

3. Detailed planning of the area, which comprised production estimates for some animal husbandry items; models of farms and villages; economic planning for villages; investments; project planning; cost-benefit studies; and an economic evaluation of the project.

4. Compilation of reports on the detailed studies and projects, discussion and preparation of the exercise; presentation of the exhibits and of the project for public discussion and evaluation.

The "final product" of the exercise included, apart from production cost-benefit studies for 20 items, a detailed settlement project, a macroplan of the valley, maps for physical planning and surveys of soil or for regional planning, the parceling of six settlements, a plan for water supply for the area, a plan for supplying electricity to the area, models for the parceling of a village, a model of a rural services center, and a model of a home plot for a settler.

The course was considered so notable a success by the Brazilians that it was soon decided to initiate a second one in mid-1972. Among the changes introduced in the second course was its extension from six to seven months to permit a more detailed study of macroprojecting.

If CIARA in Venezuela is a valid precedent, it may be assumed that these courses will be the basis for a permanent center of regional planning in Brazil.

Comprehensive Rural Development Projects

Thus far the projects examined may be classified either as specialized—different types of farms—or as rural economic—training and research institutions for comprehensive regional development. Following Israel's participation in a rural comprehensive development project in Burma in 1955, numerous other projects abroad were carried out. There was no set, accepted model for these projects. Each differed from the others according to specific needs and conditions. Their common feature was the assumption that modernization of the traditional village and of rural society requires a coordinated effort by both farmers and governments to unite agrotechnical development with rural industrialization and to create adequate economic, social, and cultural services. No project of this nature can be planned for an individual village, so the required services must be provided on a regional basis. A project of wider and more sophisticated character can be created only by the participation of professionals in various diciplines—agronomists, economists, architects, and sociologists—at every stage in its development.

In a broad sense the comprehensive regional projects in which Israeli experts have participated fall into two categories. The first, fewer in number, were projects where new villages were planned and established. They offered ample scope for the physical planner who was limited only by topography and not by existing conditions of layout, buildings, roads, and division of land. The second, greater in number, were those where planners were limited by existing villages, property divisions, irrigation systems, and generally accepted and deep-rooted habits. In addition to these problems they had to evolve methods for introducing new and comprehensive institutions for achieving desired results.

Opportunities in the first category are limited. They are usually the result of a natural or political upheaval, such as the earthquake in the Ghazvin area of Iran in 1965, when hundreds of villages were destroyed and a large-scale regional plan was imperative. The Israeli consulting firm TAHAL was commissioned to prepare and supervise two projects for the area, by far the biggest comprehensive development project abroad in which an Israeli institution has ever participated.

Among the projects arising from a political upheaval was that in the Dominican Republic after the fall of Trujillo, when several state farms were abandoned. At El Sisal, in the Dominican province of Azua, Israel assisted in developing a new regional project that included the establishment of several villages and the rehabilitation of an old port.

There are also projects growing out of large engineering changes, such as the erection of a dam that will raise the level of a river and flood villages, thereby necessitating the relocation of their population and, in the process, creating an opportunity for rural regional projects from the bottom up. Still others grow out of the feeling of obligation by the government toward specific groups, such as army veterans. New lands are set aside and funds provided for their settlement by these groups. Israel was approached several times to assist in plans for the settlement of ex-soldiers. Successful examples are the projects Tenguel and Cayambê, Ecuador.

Obviously this type of operation requires the allocation of considerable funds. As a result only such projects as can muster continuing political support on a sufficiently high level stand a chance of successful implementation. A case in point is a project carried out in a certain country where, at the request of the central government, Israel prepared a comprehensive regional development project. The experts generated enthusiasm and dedication in local authorities, and a well-adapted plan was quickly approved and executed. This plan served as a model for surrounding countries. However, the plan was never implemented in the country where it was conceived. The Israeli experts experienced a change of heart by the government when the political situation changed. The allocation of a budget to implement the planning was at first provisionally delayed and later delayed *sine die*. It was then discovered that the personnel originally designated to carry out the operation had been changed, the project was dropped from a list of priorities, and the budget allocated elsewhere.

Unexpected changes in plans and shifts in priorities because of political change are universal phenomena that cannot be avoided and must be borne in mind. This served as a lesson for Israeli experts. As a project is being prepared, and during its implementation, experts are cautioned to point out the need of assuring, as far as possible in advance, the provision of continuing institutional support. Therefore, such projects should be, as far as feasible, in a noncontroversial area, one of high priority from a national point of view and with high potential for creating continuous wide interest and impact. If an international institution, such as a regional development bank, participates in the project, the probability of continuing national support is undoubtedly greater.

Even after securing the preconditions for a successful comprehensive project, there still remains the most important ingredient—the human factor. Comprehensive projects require skills in agrotechnical fields and in organizational capacity, even in the villages themselves. Establishment of rural centers calls for people with even higher skills to provide the economic, social, and cultural services for three to five villages with 80-100 families in each. The planning of such projects and continuing professional support requires personnel with academic education. Shortage of professionals in rural areas is acute even in developed countries, let alone developing ones, where the contrast between rural and urban areas is greater. There is, of course, the need to educate such professionals from among the young people of local origin and to foster feelings of natural attachment to the regions of their birth. This is a slow process. The crucial shortage of personnel for development projects is perhaps the chief factor in curtailing such activity.

In discussions with the Inter-American Development Bank on projects in which Israeli experts were involved, officials expressed general satisfaction but expressed disappointment with what they considered the limited scale of the projects and their comparatively slow rate of growth. In response the Israelis pointed out the limitations of manpower. Planning for larger-scale projects that would outstrip manpower potential would only be self-defeating. Thus the beginnings must be in small units and simultaneous efforts must be made toward the training of development personnel at various levels. Even in those projects with apparent overall success there is a shortage of sufficiently trained people to fill the top positions.

Modernization of Agriculture

Because of the complexity of issues and the high costs of creating comprehensive projects involving the development of new areas and the establishment of new regions, major efforts are directed toward projects for the modernization of existing regions. Comprehensive rural projects with official Israeli participation in 1968 included 2 projects in Africa, 7 in Asia, and 13 in Latin America. Most of these were planned to serve a minimum of 300 families employed in agriculture and an additional number of families employed in the services center located between villages. In a few cases the outcomes fell short of the plans and the number of families in the project was smaller. In 7 of the 22 projects, however, the number of families was at least 1,000 and some were planned for as many as 3,000 families.[13]

Ghazvin, Iran. The largest project in which Israelis have participated to date, the one in Iran, was commissioned by the government of Iran and the FAO directly from the Israeli government-owned corporation of consultants, TAHAL. The Ghazvin project, begun after the disastrous earthquake of 1962, has two parts. One, commissioned by FAO, calls for a plan to restore the water supply and irrigation of the area. The other, commissioned by the Plan Organization of the government of Iran, has to do with a comprehensive plan for the rural development of the affected area. The region occupies an area of some 3,800 square kilometers (1,460 square miles) and has a rural population of 22,000 families in some 220 villages and a town, Ghazvin, of 90,000 inhabitants, in its center. The size and scope of the project necessitated the prolonged presence of a large multidiscipline team of Israelis. The success of the project is in no small part due to the Iranian authorities, who trained and prepared a suitable national group to gradually take responsibility for the project. From more than 50 Israeli experts in 1969, the number had declined to about 15 at the beginning 1972, and by the end of that year almost all of them terminated their assignments. At the last stage most of the Israeli expertise was concentrated on problems of marketing and credit and on the structuring of an adequate organizational setup, based to some extent on the model of the family-farm villages (*moshav*) in Israel.

The economics of the project demonstrated several impressive results. Between 1962 and 1966 preliminary studies and detailed plans were prepared, presented, and approved; and in 1966 actual development projects began. Between 1966 and 1971, at the end of the first stage of development, many changes had occurred. The irrigated area had increased from 2,600 hectares to 23,000 hectares; the number of wells from 95 to 272; field crops from 5,500 hectares to 20,600; and deciduous irrigated fruit trees from 910 hectares to 1,630. The yield in tons per hectare increased in wheat cultivation from 0.75 to 3.00, and in record yields up to 4.40; sugarbeet from 12.00 to 33.00, and in record yields 52.00; tomatoes from 9.00 to 32.20, and in record yields 45.00.

The average income per family increased from $180 per year to $370. It is expected that by 1975 the average yearly income will meet the target of $620 per family of six.

The very size of this project presented a challenge for Israel because of the shortage of proper manpower to fill the necessary positions abroad. This presented another problem. A large concentration of foreign experts always provides a climate for jealousy on the part of nationals who feel that they can fill the posts occupied by foreigners. It can safely be assumed, therefore, that in the future Israeli firms will accept projects calling for smaller teams abroad.

Kafulafuta and Kafubu, Zambia. The Kafulafuta and Kafubu Farmer's Cooperative Settlement Schemes, in Copperbelt Province, are considered outstanding achievements of Zambia's rural development program. Each consists of three cooperative villages based on family farming, with a rural union center providing economic, social, and cultural services for the surrounding villages.

Both schemes were planned for a total of 900 agricultural families, with 200 additional to be employed in the rural centers. Their gradual and organic growth can prove the suitability of the underlying economic and organizational concepts. The response of the farmers was, on the whole, excellent; and their achievements in irrigation, livestock production, and organization of marketing surpassed the original planning targets.

By the end of 1971 some 500 agricultural families were settled and another 50 were in service centers. The investment costs per holding averaged $1,800, and the yearly income per family was $450. This ratio of 4:1 between investment and yearly income is considered satisfactory.

The present types of farm units in the villages were decided upon after several years of experimentation with different crops and animal husbandry. In addition, the difference between the villages also reflects the differences of topographical and geographical conditions, such as availability of water for irrigation.

The social objectives of the plan aimed at creating cohesive units with a firm basis for community life. For that purpose the basic condition was created by assuring that all farmers have their housing no more than three kilometers from the rural center.

The Israeli team of experts worked with the development of the scheme from various angles: physical planning, economic planning, experimentation with crops, animal husbandry, accounting, organization, and marketing. Courses were held to provide knowledge of the more complex economic and agricultural issues. Special emphasis was placed on ensuring maximal support and cooperation by the official local authorities and other relevant institutions, both economic and social, in the neighboring town, Luanshia.

The president of Zambia, Kenneth Kaunda, praised both schemes during his visit to the area in 1971 saying: "This is an achievement which deserves the admiration of the country as a whole . . . here we may be pretty close to finding the answer to grassroots development for which we have been searching since independence" (*Zambia Farmer*, August 18, 1971).

These were very gratifying words coming from the chief of state. Israeli experts referred to them in drawing attention of the responsible authorities to conditions for the continuing prosperity of the scheme. Most of them refer to the need for continuing development, first until completion of its original dimension—1,000 agricultural families and 200 in services—and later, of developing of similar schemes in the vicinity. A bigger unit, of several thousand families, will justify setting up regional services, such as factories and plants for the processing of agricultural products, schools, clinics, and community centers. Only when several schemes like the present one develop into a larger, comprehensive region will they become viable with the potential for successful growth.

El Sisal.   The El Sisal settlement project in the Dominican Republic presents a very interesting case of development methodology. It was planned and executed in a very difficult political situation when the country faced prolonged tension and civil war. However, it enjoyed the central government's continuing interest in its progress. This, of course, was one of the essential conditions for its success.

The project comprises a large-scale training farm—*Finca Escuela*—on what was previously a sisal farm belonging to Trujillo, adjacent to some 8 villages for 500 agricultural families and a rural center, according to present plans. Additional plans call for industrial enterprises and the reconstruction of a small port.

The farm offered immediate employment for 100 laborers and it acquainted laborers with modern agriculture and allowed the farm managers to conduct experiments necessary for establishing optimal types of farms in the settlement. After working for two agricultural seasons, the laborers were settled in the new villages and became independent farmers. The training farm then received new candidates for settlement.

The actual work on the farm was started in 1967. The first settlers took possession of their plots in the new settlement in 1969. In 1970 there were almost 200 laborers in the *Finca Escuela* and an equal number in the settlements. Later in the year, when the president officially inaugurated the project, the settlers had already received their homes; and in the rural center the construction of a church and a number of public buildings had been completed.

The economics of the project exceeded planning and expectations.[14] The average yearly income of an agricultural laborer in the area was about $200. The laborers in the *Finca Escuela El Sisal* were being paid $400 out of current farm income. The first two agricultural seasons showed gross income of an individual farmer in the settlement project of $4,000 instead of the planned $3,000—the net income was $1,500 instead of the planned $1,200. These figures must still be considered as tentative until additional data for following years are available.

The successful progress of the project was due to a variety of factors. In the first place, a group of Dominican professionals and technicians became involved in its initial planning. Their enthusiasm and dedication became the guidelines of the project. During their visit to Israel in 1965 they became familiar with details of the organization and operation of cooperative villages. Simultaneous with the actual planning of *El Sisal*, a course for comprehensive rural planning was conducted. The Dominican Agrarian Institute provided the project with continuing and enthusiastic support. Initial success facilitated financial operations and the Dominican Agrarian Bank expressed readiness to offer credit. The facilties of agriculture of the republic's two universities showed active interest in the project and used it to demonstrate the operations of a successful rural project.

The study conducted by Naor and Regev considers that *El Sisal* 's greatest merit is its providing clear proof that there is the possibility of developing modern agriculture under adverse climatic and soil conditions, and of transforming the *campesinos* (villagers) from passive participants in a poor economy into active, productive, and successful farmers who deserve respect and support.

On the other hand, the study indicates that the heavy costs, especially in the allocation of technical assistance (180 man-months of Israeli experts), was excessive in relation to the number of families who benefited from the scheme. In the circumstances how could anyone suggest a similar procedure for the 400,000 families subsisting on agriculture in the Dominican Republic? Therefore *El Sisal* must be considered an investment in the general process of modernization of agriculture in the Dominican Republic. Forthcoming projects drawing on its experience will have to be considerably less costly in terms of both manpower and money. *El Sisal* and its continuing development are interesting from the viewpoint of development methodology.

Vientiane Plains, Laos. Of a completely different nature is the comprehensive project in Laos. An Israeli team was requested for assistance in two projects on the Vientiane Plains. At the Nam-Ngum experimental farm new technologies were tried out, including new seed varieties—especially the "miracle rice" (IRRI C4-63, mentioned in the report of the Mekong River Committee)—new crops, and new farm implements. In the comprehensive village nearby, encompassing some 20 villages with a population of approximately 3,000 families, the objective is to introduce gradual changes, converting each village into a multipurpose agricultural cooperative. The first step in this direction was to organize for the introduction of proper irrigation so as to ensure two crops of rice annually. Previously the villages cultivated rice only once a year, after the seasonal floods submerged the land to be used. At the suggestion of Israeli experts, water for the irrigation needed for a second crop was paid for by the inhabitants of the villages through their own organization, without seeking aid of the Ministry of Agriculture. The money raised was used for a lift pump. The 1969 report of the Mekong River Committee cites the fact that the villagers learned to regard water as a commodity that must be paid for.[15]

Following the successful introduction of a second crop through irrigation, steps were taken to provide the Nam-Ngum cooperative project with joint marketing and joint purchase of inputs. Constant attention is also given to the improvement of extension services.

Comprehensive Planning

Before ending the discussion of Israeli performance in the complex field of comprehensive projects, attention should be focused on the great variety and the different typologies involved in this category. They include both planning and actual implementation advice. They are performed both by official Israeli international cooperation programs and by independent Israeli consultants. Some years ago comprehensive projects concentrated predominantly on rural society; but recently they have added urban aspects, since both are considered to be components of comprehensive regional planning. Industrial plants in rural areas and in development towns receive ever-growing attention. On several occasions there have been discussions with Latin American institutions regarding the possibility of joint studies on urban-rural relationships in Latin America.

A project of comprehensive planning in Crete, undertaken by an Israeli group of experts on behalf of the Organization for Economic Cooperation and Development (OECD) was completed in the early 1960s. Crete's proximity to Israel made possible the use of a great many specialists for relatively short assignments. Many recommendations were quickly implemented in various fields, including agriculture, irrigation, tourism, vocational training, and other services. The success of the project was generally recognized by both the central and local authorities of Greece and the OECD. When the project was terminated, informal contacts for aid and consultation continued and served as another proof of the effectiveness of the project.[16]

Comprehensive planning in its entirety was the subject of a Rehovot Conference in 1963.[17] It presented an opportunity for professionals and academic people to confront and consult politicians and field executives on a pragmatic level, in order to examine the similarities and differences between approaches to rural planning throughout the world. While the Rehovot Conference of 1971 dealt chiefly with urbanization much attention was given to problems of comprehensive planning.

NOTES

1.   For detailed discussion of comprehensive planning see Raanan Weitz and Avshalom Rokah, *Agricultural Development, Planning and Implementation, Israel Case Study* (Dodrecht, Netherlands: D. Reidel, 1968); and Raanan Weitz, *From Peasant to Farmer, A Revolutionary Strategy for Development* (New York and London: XX Century Fund, Columbia University Press, 1971).

2. Emmanuel Yalan et al., *The Modernization of Traditional Agricultural Villages, Minority Villages in Israel* (Rehovot: Settlement Study Centre, 1972).

3. Ministry for Foreign Affairs, International Cooperation Division, and Ministry of Agriculture, Centre for Agricultural Cooperation, *Israel's Agricultural Cooperation with Developing Countries* (Jerusalem: the Ministries, April 1970), pp. 11 ff.

4. Ibid., p. 14.

5. Gideon Naor and Shaul Regev, *Seed Multiplication Project in Nordeste of Brazil* (Rehovot: Settlement Study Centre, October 1970), provisional report in Hebrew.

6. Ibid., p. 48, quoted from a conversation with the former Israel ambassador, Yossef Nahmias.

7. Ministry for Foreign Affairs, International Cooperation Division, and Ministry of Agriculture, Centre for Agricultural Cooperation, op. cit., p. 24.

8. Ibid., p. 37.

9. Gideon Naor and Shaul Regev, *Israel Cooperation Projects in Venezuela* (Rehovot: Settlement Study Centre, 1971), provisional draft in Hebrew.

10. Ibid., p. 108.

11. Ibid., p. 58.

12. Ibid., p. 54.

13. Ministry for Foreign Affairs, International Cooperation Division, and Ministry of Agriculture, Centre for Agricultural Cooperation, op. cit., p. 38.

14. Gideon Naor and Shaul Regev, *"El Sisal," in Dominican Republic* (Rehovot; Settlement Study Centre, 1970), provisional draft in Hebrew, p. 22.

15. *Annual Report of the Committee for the Coordination of Investigations of the Lower Mekong Basin, E/CN 11/WRD/MKG/L.298; E/CN 11/901* (Bangkok: Economic Commission for Asia and the Far East, 1969), pp. 76-77.

16. A. Rosenman, *Crete: Agricultural Development of Four Selected Regions* (Tel Aviv: Agridev, 1966).

17. *Rural Planning in Developing Countries, Report on the Second Rehovot Conference, Israel, August 1963* (London: Routledge and Paul, 1965).

5

YOUTH PROGRAMS

Because of the continually accelerating rhythm of change in society, in both developed and developing countries, we are faced with an enormous challenge in the education of youth. Not only must such education help youth to accept basic social and national values, it must also ensure the identification of and involvement of the younger generation in the development of ideals and policies. Simultaneously youth education must assure the assimilation of changes brought about by accepted technological innovations. Unless these challenges are met satisfactorily, the danger of estrangement of youth and the growth of dissident cultures, destructive of existing national and social goals, looms large.

In developing countries two factors make the problem even more acute. The first is the very high proportion of young people in relation to the entire population, and the second is the more rapid and more drastic character of the changes that must be faced in the transition from patterns of traditional society to those of modern society. In 1971 the ratio of people under the age of 20 in developing countries was more than 50 percent, while in developed countries it was only 35 percent. In Africa the ratio was even higher, reaching 55 percent.

Youth in developing countries must face many conflicts, the chief of which is that of "two groups of bodies aspiring to centrality in the society;"[1] the new political entity—the state as a sovereign body with powers of enforcement, as opposed to the traditional tribe, village, or region. The goal for those responsible for the education of youth is the development of young people's civic responsibility and active participation in the modern political system—and, at the same time, the conservation of patterns of loyalty to the village, tribe, and region, whenever such loyalties can be successfully established.

The function of that elementary social unit, the family, is also undergoing change. In this situation every available tool in addition to formal education must be used to channel the energies and aspirations of young people into creative outlets. Educational programs of various kinds play an important role, and youth movements and organizations have a prominent place among them. They can contribute greatly toward the creation of a useful youth culture that can help the young to become a socializing factor in a society that is changing rapidly. "Youth is the meeting point and the inter-generation point of transfer, and for this reason youth culture can serve as the principal meeting point for the longstanding aims of society on one hand, and inclinations and processes of social change on the other."[2]

In Israel's own history, youth movements played a prominent part. The several stages and patterns of these movements had a profound effect on the programs in which Israel's experts participated abroad.

Although Israeli youth movements had their roots in those of Europe of the late nineteenth or early twentieth centuries, they were basically different in character. They were not merely protest movements in opposition to adult society, with a sizable dose of Rousseauism and despair of human society mixed with idealization of anarchistic patterns of individualism. Israeli youth movements were protests against the existing patterns that limited Jewish life both in the Diaspora and in Palestine. They combined recreational activities, such as scouting, indoor games, and song fests, with ideological education in discussing and developing opinions on political issues and—more difficult—in laying the basis and strengthening the motivation for future "self-realization" of ideals in adult life. From their very beginnings each of these movements set a precise scale of values, differing in details but basically uniform in concentration on performance of pioneering functions in building the country, in defense, and in the establishment of a society inspired by ideals of social justice. Perhaps, to put it another way, the central normative concept was pioneerism; and its concrete expression was a situation where young men and women left their middle-class homes, studies, and patterns of existence in the Diaspora to come to Israel and form collective settlements, to work on roads, or to do other hard, physically exhausting labor and to participate in defense organization. Among the youth movements in Palestine, some were devoted to working youth, others to studying youth, and some included both.

Although it might sound pretentious, those hundreds of thousands who belonged to the youth movements, even if they did not join an agricultural settlement after they reached their majority, or spent only a short time there, shared for a time a justified belief that they actually participated in the process of nation-building and practicing one of its basic precepts of self-realization.

An institution in the history of Israel's educational process is the Youth Aliya —the Youth Immigration organization. Originally established in the early 1930s to save Jewish children from Nazi-dominated countries in Europe, it developed into an admirable organization that offered homes, mainly in agricultural collectives, cooperative settlements, or in special educational institutions, to tens of thousands of young people aged 14 to 18 who arrived in Israel without families or who were native Israelis who could not stay with their families. The organization developed a pattern of continuing work and studies in the settlements, supervised and assisted by a body of professional teachers and social instructors. Many groups of graduates of the Youth Aliya established new settlements or became otherwise involved in the development of the state. Undoubtedly membership in youth movements has had a lasting effect on the individuals in Israeli society.

In the years just preceding Israel's statehood, and during the early years of the state, two national youth organizations achieved prominence—Gadna and Nahal. Gadna (*Gedudey Noar*, Youth Formations), founded in 1940, engaged youth aged 14-16 (later up to 18) in physical and paramilitary training combined with scouting, education in civics, and fostering of social values. The program included weekly lessons and field days once a month, but the focuses were on the yearly national service camps and excursions and cross-country marches.

Nahal (*Noar Halutzi Lochem*, Fighting Pioneer Youth) is an integral part of the army. It was formed shortly after the establishment of the state for the graduates of youth movements who intended to join old settlements or establish new ones. According to a pattern established since then, they are able to enlist together in the army, alternating periods of military training with work in established agricultural settlements or in the new border settlements. While enlisting was obligatory under the law of military service, joining the Nahal was voluntary. The special interest of members of Nahal in becoming paratroopers demonstrated that they excelled not only in settlement and in agriculture but also in military functions. Upon completion of their army service they are given four choices: a) continuing as farmers, members of the kibbutz in which they worked; b) of forming or joining a new settlement; c) of taking up another occupation; or d) of starting university studies. Usually the choice was new settlements in the border areas.

All countries that requested Israeli advice on youth programs had such programs, usually sponsored by the state, frequently by religious or professional groups, and sometimes by a voluntary service. Israeli advisors were inspired by their own diversified experience. They offered a selection of organizational and conceptual elements that combined the youth culture and social ideals of youth movements with Youth Aliya's formal education and work; Gadna's physical training and national and civic education; and Nahal's pioneering civilian and military service. Each country faced its own needs, arising from the differing backgrounds of youth programs, and consequently adapted the programs suggested by Israeli advisors that were most suited to their needs.

The professional agency that provided guidance for the above projects until 1971 was the Department of International Cooperation in the Ministry of Defense. The first requests for cooperation specified an interest in the Gadna and Nahal types of activities, and the Israeli expertise in this field was concentrated in the Ministry of Defense. Since there is no Ministry for Youth in the Israeli administration, and in order to avoid duplication, the Department of International Cooperation was charged with assisting all youth programs, although the majority were completely civilian in character. In 1972 a new independent center was created for directing international cooperation in youth programs, with no ties to the Ministry of Defense. It is one of the activities financed and coordinated by the Division for International Cooperation. Its director is assisted by a board of specialists drawn from ministries and university departments. The center is responsible for the coordination and pedagogical guidance of a variety of extracurricular and nonconventional modalities of youth activities, both urban and rural. It is expected that in the future it will be in a better position to offer for application abroad the cumulative experience of Israelis in diversified youth movement activities.

Of the 19 projects abroad in 1971, 13 were conducted in Africa and 6 in Latin

America. In Asia, Israel participated in Singapore for several years and in 1970 received requests for advising on the organization of national youth programs in Thailand and the Philippines.

The programs in Africa dealt mainly with rural populations. Those in towns were directed primarily to secondary-school students and concentrated on civic education and physical training for a number of hours weekly. A basic study, covering three African countries, classified the organizational patterns of the programs according to the criteria of "the degree of control over the members' activities exercised by the movement and the center."[3] It lists three broad categories:

1.   Activities in which the movement has "complete and intensive control." These include for the most part prolonged courses (six months to a year) at training farms and bases. The trainees acquire skills in agriculture, in trades (carpentry, mechanics, building), in education in civics, literacy, general knowledge, and in a few cases the elements of paramilitary training.

2.   Activities in which the movement exercises only a limited amount of control, such as new villages or traditional adopted villages to which members of the movement return after leaving the training centers.

3.   Activities with a very loose control by the movement. Here the functions of the movement are limited to a specific number of hours weekly. The members of the movement did not in the past have any opportunity to spend a prolonged period under the guidance of the movement. Two prototypes of this category might serve the rural clubs in the villages and the Gadna-type classes in secondary schools in towns. Both are engaged mainly in educational functions, with emphasis on literacy in rural clubs and on civics and national education in urban secondary schools.

The first category is the most likely to have a lasting effect on its graduates, but at the same time it is the most difficult for the state to carry out on a major scale because it requires a substantial budget to maintain the trainees for a lengthy period. It also requires a great deal of qualified manpower during its formation, and this might oblige the state to lean heavily on foreign advisors. Of course, the idea of using the army in part for civilian, peaceful, and constructive duties is very attractive. Apart from the better utilization of actual manpower, the pioneer movements inspired by Nahal can have a far-reaching and educationally symbolic effect by spreading a prophetic ideal: "And they shall beat their swords into ploughshares."

Over a period of time one can come to several conclusions regarding the use of the army for peaceful purposes. The stay in a training farm should not exceed one year. Past experience has shown that longer periods—some up to three years—created serious problems for ex-servicemen. Their stay in the army for longer periods, in an agricultural or other training depot, under conditions much superior to those in their villages often made return to their homes very difficult; indeed, the majority did not return but drifted toward towns, often increasing unemployment. A relatively minor problem facing the organizers was the question of fixed wages or pocket money.[4] Though the sums are small, the use of money as an incentive in youth service is questionable.

A most important preoccupation is obviously the manning of administrative and educational staffs. Sometimes teachers are used as instructors, but the experience is not always successful. Teachers tend to impart formal discipline and create a school atmosphere. Youth instructors should create a spirit of comradeship and use it as a medium for achieving the aims sought.

In all forms of youth activity the elements of service, usefulness, and purpose-fulness of the organization must be incorporated. In Europe, the cradle of the youth movement idea, decline came about because the movement did not develop into an instrument with a well-defined, purposeful activity. Sometimes it evolved into the youth section of a political party—usually the opposition party—or, in a dictatorial, one-party system it degenerated into the nationalistic, parade-happy offspring of the government party. The youth revolution movements, during the 1960s in Europe and in the United States, in their different varieties, bear witness to the complexity of the problem and to the inadequacy of relevant solutions in developed countries. All are perturbed by the generation gap and the lack of creative feedback between the scale values of the managing generation and those who follow.

The challenge that faces all of us, then, is similar. In the developing countries it becomes even more complex. There the goal is "the development of civic responsibility, participatory political culture. The individual considers himself an active part of the political system and is oriented toward relating to all groups in the political system."[5] The youth groups, when able to achieve these goals, can assist meaningfully in the processes of building a "value and cultural infrastructure common to all members of the society as well as defining the feeling of belonging of the individual to the new collective, a feeling which goes beyond the formal contractual link, committing him as a citizen to the new state center."[6]

In projects with Israeli participation, efforts were made to find concrete expression for the identification of the youth movement with national and societal goals. Whenever possible, especially in greater national movements, members, upon completion of their regular service, were requested to return to their villages or to form new ones to help fulfill the objectives of the movement. In cases where participants spent only a short time in camp, even when their activities were only extracurricular, some concrete function for fulfilling a real need of the community was identified.

In Lesotho the problem of land erosion is critical, and every year extended areas of arable land are destroyed. Lesotho's youth movement, active in farm training centers in rural areas, took part in programs combating erosion. In Chad members of the local *Jeunesse Pionière* participated in afforestation projects, undertaken on a large scale in conjunction with the FAO. In Costa Rica the national youth movement was active in the rural areas in the form of voluntary clubhouses, and its activities included volunteer work camps. In each region the type of function assigned was determined by local needs.

At several international meetings the question was presented as to whether activities of "export" (or foreign) volunteers should be independent of or coordinat-ed with ongoing development projects assisted by national and international agencies. It was always the opinion of the Israeli delegates that to be really effective, such activities must be fully coordinated with local development projects. Apart from concentration of efforts, because of tremendous and ever-growing needs in developing countries, coordination of volunteer projects with ongoing development programs would promote identification and participation of youth in the process of national and international development, and avoid estrangement or apathy.

Anyone active in youth programs realizes that the problems and challenges are tremendous and constantly growing. The greatest problem is unemployment, which becomes particularly acute when accompanied by a rural exodus. This leads to pockets of poverty, misery, and marginal living conditions. Rehabilitation of youth in urban areas is much more difficult and costly than the outlay necessary to prevent or limit a rural exodus.

Israel has only limited experience in urban youth activities abroad, apart from the Gadna-type programs in secondary schools. Some successful projects were carried out in vocational training on a part-time basis in Tanzania. Two reasons for the success of this activity were the combination of actual employment in industry with theoretical training and previous participation in youth movements. Perhaps these two factors should serve as general guidelines for youth programs in urban areas. Isolated vocational training does not fill a real need and does not offer a concrete solution unless suitable employment is secured as a result. In the second place, employment by itself is not enough. Youth must be provided with the proper motivation and adequate social and national value scales generated by youth movements. Perhaps the greatest challenge for the development community of the world today is to provide in each region, according to its needs, the appropriate organizational and administrative conditions and the machinery required to create adequate employment opportunities for urban youth, at the same time enabling it to enjoy sufficient time for supplementary vocational training and cultural and civic education. A type of urban Youth Aliya, along the lines mentioned above, would seem the answer to this challenge. The expenditure necessary for this type of activity would be considerable, but its success is possible only if governments are willing to give it the high priority it deserves.

NOTES

1. Quoted in R. Shapira and Y. Oren, *Contribution of Youth to Development of the State* (Jerusalem Division for International Cooperation, 1970), p. 3.

2. Quoted in ibid., p. 10.

3. R. Shapira *et al.*, *Israel Assistance to African Countries—Youth Programmes* (in Hebrew), quoted in ibid., p. 27.

4. P. Gonen, "Principles of Organization of National Services and Youth Movements" (1972), provisional manuscript, in Hebrew.

5. Shapira and Oren, op. cit., p. 4.

6. Ibid., p. 35.

The term "community development" has various, sometimes diametrically opposite, meanings in current jargon or literature. In Israeli practice its generally accepted connotation refers to steps taken to activate a community for self-help and advancement: finding solutions to problems, solutions inspired by the process of self-government, the promotion of leadership, and respect for traditions compatible with the modernization of the economic structure and the promotion of self-esteem.

In a more restricted sense, in the practice of its international cooperation the term has been used by Israel to denote activities tending to incorporate women in the process of development. It is almost a truism in Israeli projects at home and abroad that it is impossible to achieve meaningful development without concentrated efforts to involve the women and the families of a community. The reason for these efforts is not only that women constitute half of the total adult population but also that their function in the education of children at home, and in social services generally, is vitally important. In many of the developing nations the condition of women—their social status—particularly in terms of equal access to education, vocational training, and employment, has given a sense of urgency to the need to change prevailing social attitudes toward them and their rightful role in national progress.

In the history of the Jewish national and political movements, the problem of the emancipation of women never appeared acute. Women, after all, participated in these movements most actively from their very inception and occupied positions of leadership. In agricultural settlements, in work formations, and in other areas women insisted on equal rights, even on the chance of performing physical work, no matter what hardship might be involved, including the plowing of virgin soil and the construction of roads, as well as doing highly professional and executive work. Even in such pioneering, not to say dangerous, challenges as self-defense women participated with a will. Underlying all of their efforts for recognition and the right of full participation has been their desire for full partnership in overall progress, without exception in any field of service to their state.

This approach by the women of developing nations helped to inspire the cooperative projects undertaken by the Mount Carmel Center for Community Development.* The origins of this program can be traced back to the U.N. Conference held in Addis Ababa in 1960, a conference that specifically discussed the issue of women's role in developing countries, with stress on ways in which they might become full partners in progress. Several specific areas were highlighted in which women might play a predominant role, among them the challenging area of conquering illiteracy. Because of Israel's experience in confronting this and other problems of development, a seminar in Israel was suggested to discuss the role of women in a developing society. The response to invitations to this seminar was enthusiastic. Sixty-six participants, many of them veterans of the Addis Ababa conference, arrived from Asia, Africa, and the Mediterranean countries. The seminar, which included systematic visits to development projects, women's organizations, and educational and social institutions, lasted for six weeks. At its completion participants recommended the creation in Israel of a permanent institute for the training of women and the establishment abroad of a center for community development with Israel's advice and participation. Pursuant to these recommendations the Mount Carmel International Training Center for Community Services (MCTC) was established in Haifa. In Machakos, Kenya, Israel was active for many years in establishing and administering a school for social workers; this school was later incorporated into the Kenya Institute of Administration.

The MCTC was founded in 1961 with the participation of the Joint Body of the Cooperative Guild, the Women's Section of the Trade Unions, and the Social Democratic Federation of Women in Sweden, which have participated ever since on its board of directors. The Swedish government itself became interested in the activities of the MCTC and offered scholarships to women from Africa enrolled in its courses.

During the Center's first ten years (1961-71) more than 1,500 have participated in its courses and seminars, conducted chiefly in education, food technology, nutrition, and handicrafts. In education emphasis has been placed on both nursery and kindergarten and adult courses, all based on the community development approach. This method and emphasis reflect Israeli preoccupation with the specific, indispensable role women can and should play in community development. It also manifests the Israeli concept of the essential nature of education, not as a limited formal process but as a continuum encompassing the life of man from early childhood to maturity. The need to provide for such continuing education has become both more urgent and more obvious, given the increasing rate of change and readaptation to change in all areas of life. Kindergarten training is clearly a *sine qua non* of organic growth in mental development and potential through the formative and early adult years. Adult education, particularly the conquest of illiteracy, is a precondition of productive adult participation in economic and social development.

---

*Basic data appear in a short pamphlet issued by the Center on its tenth anniversary (April 1971).

Courses in handicrafts, home industries, and cooperative marketing have focused both on the development of skills and on problems of economics and organization. Participants learn techniques of increasing production, adapting traditional designs and patterns, and marketing to increase their earning capacity.

MCTC has also developed a methodology of training essential to ascertaining the learning level of its participants and the time required for their instruction. The courses, which last from four to six months, are planned for middle-level personnel charged with teaching and supervisory functions. They combine actual learning techniques and teaching methods with extended observation of methods employed in Israel. For students with higher executive training and responsibility, study tours of shorter duration—from four to six weeks—are conducted. These special courses do not include formal studies but are geared mainly to enabling participants to gain the widest possible view of the Israeli approach to a subject. Such study tours covered social welfare services, nonconventional approaches to education, and out-of-school youth projects. Seminars, usually held biennially and also of short duration (two to three weeks), are conducted for participants from Africa and Latin America who perform central functions in their respective professions. These seminars, also attended by representatives of international women's organizations, are devoted to the examination of a relatively broad subject, such as the role of voluntary organizations in the development of a community or social and cultural integration in urban areas. The exchange of information is of great value. A symposium held in April 1971 to mark 10 years of the MCTC's activities brought together women from 20 countries who had attended at least one of the previous seven seminars. They assessed the programs and discussed the changing needs in the education of women for the second development decade.

A meeting held in June 1972, convened by the Division of Social Development of the U.N. Secretariat in conjunction with the Section on the Status of Women of the U.N. Division of Human Rights, examined means of advancing integration of women in general national struggles for development. It has been an intrinsic part of Israeli doctrine in all past projects to stress the need for the involvement of women in such struggles. This emphasis began in rural societies, which still form the greater part of the population in developing countries. Clearly educational facilities for women must be increased not only to raise their status but also to ease their absorption into developmental efforts. The Israeli delegate to the 1972 conference made this point clear. Pursuant to the recommendations of the conference, additional courses to meet this need were advocated to supplement community services. It was also recommended that training facilities in agriculture and the vocational arts for girls be increased as much as possible.

Participants in courses in Israel are always requested to indicate what impressed them most during their visit to the country. Most commonly cited among characteristics of Israeli life is the nation's hard, dedicated work. This observation is perhaps in itself justification for conducting the courses in Israel as well as in the receiving country. It is a truism, but nonetheless true, that actions speak louder than words. When a trainee, in Israel or elsewhere, sees "development in action," an ideal realized in the concrete, he is in a position of greater strength—not to say inspiration —when he returns home to apply his newly acquired skills and ideas.

In recent years the MCTC has begun to integrate into its courses themselves practical application to indigenous problems within some developing countries. What is now called "in-country" training has been conducted in Iran in adult education, in Zambia in nutrition, and in Mali in kindergarten training. This innovation has proved most successful. In addition to allowing students to demonstrate the results of their studies in their home countries or on their own continent, this format, through the mere presence of students and faculty, provided an occasion for focusing a wider, national attention on a course and so contributed toward its success and acceptability. Instructors who had accompanied students through various phases of projects from concept to realization now became helpful in the more direct challenge of "replanting" their graduates in their native soil, facing concrete, indigenous problems.

It is to be hoped that the continuation of in-country training as a supplement to courses in Israel will give instructors of the MCTC an insight into the complexities of the challenge of developing concrete projects abroad and participating in them directly for a number of years.

It is regrettable, for example, that since Israeli participation in the Kenya-Israel School of Social Work in Machakos, later transferred to Nairobi, ended in 1970, after eight years of successful association, almost no other lasting project in community development has been assisted by Israelis. In several cases, such as Peru and Zaïre, feasibility studies were made but did not advance further. In the latter part of 1972, a successful project for the training of kindergarten supervisors and teachers began to develop in Lagos, Nigeria.

The primary reason for this failure has clearly been the difficulty of finding professional women free from family obligations and thus able to undertake long-range programs abroad. The MCTC is continuing its efforts to broaden professionally so as to be in a position to staff projects abroad more effectively, both as an extension of its work in Israel and as a greater assurance that its Israel-based courses will be realized not only in the classrooms and fields of Israel but also in the nations of the 1,500 foreign students Israel has instructed. This problem was also in the background of its interest in establishing relations with the newly created school for social workers at Haifa University. It is possible that among the students at Haifa who get to know the work of the MCTC, some will decide to choose community development abroad as their profession. Contacts with Haifa University in the course of 1972 indicated good prospects for establishing professional links between the two institutions.

7

COOPERATIVES, TRADE UNIONS, AND HISTADRUT

Israeli cooperative institutions, for the most part, differ from those in Western countries. In Israel, from the very outset, emphasis was placed on producer cooperatives rather than consumer cooperatives. The cooperative emerged as an integral part of the labor movement, striving to fulfill national and pioneering functions in the process of building the country.

John K. Galbraith observed on one of his visits to Israel that emerging societies require assistance of three kinds: capital, manpower training, and concepts. In the last two Israel's contribution might be of value. The wide range of cooperatives in Israel, and Israel's diversified application of cooperative concepts both at home and in assistance projects abroad can serve as good illustrations of this observation.

Earlier in this study it was stated that agriculture and the establishment of a rural society were given prime roles during the formative period of the national movement. In its labor movement, starting with the Second *Aliya* (wave of immigration) in 1904, a wide variety of cooperatives was developed with varying elements. There were "communes," which for quite a time practiced complete ownership of all property. At the other extreme loose, single-purpose cooperatives came into being, similar to those in the West.

The founders of the first "communes" or "collectives," forerunners of the later *kibbutz* and *moshav* types of settlements were fortunate in that those responsible for administration of national land and of budgets allocated for its settlement were sympathetic to their ideas and ready to place at their disposal the funds necessary for initial investment and revolving credit. They also proved that dealing with an organized group of settlers over a period of time had many advantages over dealing with individuals, especially since many of them were unfamiliar with the practice of agriculture.

While the prevailing type of cooperative in the labor movement was agricultural, there were other types. In the wake of World War I members of the Zionist-

46

Socialist movement who came from Eastern Europe organized the Labour Legion. There was a vast difference between this organization and the Russian prototype, the Workers Brigade. The membership of the former was completely voluntary and its leadership democratic. Its aim was to serve the emerging national movement in its civilian needs and challenges, parallel to the way the Army Legion would serve in emergencies for defense. During the early 1920s members of the Labour Legion were occupied in road building, initiated by the new British mandate government, in stone quarries, and in construction of buildings. Later it was among the founders of a new collective agricultural movement.

Simultaneous with the development of the collective type of agricultural settlement (the *kibbutz*), the smallholder type of settlement (*moshav*) evolved, creating what is currently known as a multipurpose cooperative. Each member (approximately 80-100) was given an equal start—identical plot, house, and other facilities. The individual farmer cultivates his plot, but there is a built-in provision for mutual assistance in case of need or emergency (disease or army call-up, for example). Where necessary or feasible, functions are conducted on a cooperative basis—marketing, the purchase of inputs, central water installation, use of heavy agricultural equipment, and social and cultural activities. The policy of the *moshav* is decided by a general assembly, while day-to-day business is conducted by an elected rotating committee whose members serve without pay.

Agricultural settlements have developed various countrywide institutions with the passing of time—institutions that have benefited the entire movement. At the same time they have become important pressure groups, exerting political leverage, a trend that is manifest in the preparation of lists for the Knesset and observation of officeholders in the political parties.

Among the cooperatives that originated in the workers' movement, the most successful have been the transport cooperatives. They control and perform services in urban and interurban transportation—functions performed elsewhere by local authorities or other local bodies.

Cooperative institutions were and are widely accepted in the nonlabor sector as well. A network of cooperatives of small middle-class farmers developed, performing such functions as marketing and joint puchase of inputs. Mutual societies for savings and loans were more popular during the late 1930s and early 1940s than they are now. There is also a range of cooperatives concerned with such functions as housing, purchasing, services, and marketing. The Registrar of Cooperatives listed almost 2,000 cooperatives of various types in 1971.

Evidently cooperation has been and continues to be characteristic of Israeli society. Perhaps this occurs because it allows for economy of scale in suitable operations, combined with individual control in the general policy-making process, in defining the limits of the cooperative responsibility, and in independent management of residual affairs.

LABOR

The predominant interest of the developing countries was in Israeli cooperative concepts and institutions directly related to the labor movement. From the outset the labor movement in Israel accepted responsibility for national affairs. Even in the early stages of the Zionist movement, labor leaders became national leaders who were basically interested in national issues and developed a sense of national responsibility. For example, the labor movement took on the responsibility of forming nuclei of self-defense. These later developed into the *Hagana*, the forerunner of the Israeli Defense Forces.

Another feature of the movement was the unification of approach for rural and urban workers. For a long time the labor elite was associated with the rural cooperative sector, which produced national leaders in a much higher percentage than its share of the national population. This, however, was because the labor movement from the beginning considered participation in agricultural cooperatives to be the highest expression of national aims. When Histadrut—the General Federation of Labor—was organized in 1920, this set of values had already been established. From its formation membership was open not only to employees of "capitalist" firms but also to the workers in its own establishments in collective settlements and cooperatives or in industry, transport, building, and other services of the labor-owned economy. Members of Histadrut are automatically members of the Workers Association and, as such, are the formal owners of many important establishments throughout Israel.

The pluralistic and nondoctrinaire character of Histadrut and its preoccupation with broad national issues are evidenced by the existence of enterprises owned jointly with private and public establishments.

It is difficult to list the variety of assistance projects abroad which took on important elements of a specifically Israeli brand of cooperation, trade unionism, or Histadrut ideology and structure. All agricultural projects abroad and courses related to agriculture and rural society in Israel have qualities of cooperative cultivation, marketing, and other functions. The same is true of youth and community projects. Programs for public health and social medicine in rural areas utilize the infrastructure and the "doctrine" of the *Kupat-Holim*—the sick fund of Histadrut. One is almost tempted to say that Israeli assistance projects use their Histadrut institutions and experience as a second technical language.

The following discussion, based on two training institutes in Israel and referring briefly to two projects abroad, presents only one definite aspect of activities reflecting the use of Israeli cooperation inspired by the many institutions of Histadrut.

The Afro-Asian Institute for Cooperative and Labour Studies was formally founded in 1960. By 1958 the International Department of Histadrut had already held its first Afro-Asian seminar, attended by 61 participants. The first courses were held simultaneously in English and in French. Subsequently separate courses were held every year, in English and in French—each of four months' duration. Up to the end of 1972 there were 26 regular international courses, 36 special and specific courses on request, and 24 local seminars in developing countries. The total number of participants in courses held in Israel and abroad was about 3,700, and they came from 87 countries.

The program in every course includes a minimum of lectures and a maximum of discussions and other study sessions on the following subjects: development problems in young countries—rural development, community development, public land ownership; cooperation—theory and practice, in Israel and in Africa and Asia; the labor movement—history and ideas; labor organization—labor relations, labor exchange, vocational training, and youth organization; national and social objectives of the workers' movement; and relations between trade unions and cooperative movements.

Additional subjects are examined in study groups and workshops. Detailed field excursions enable the participants to become more closely acquainted with Israeli experience in the subjects of the seminar. These include visits and work at agricultural settlements and discussions with supervisors of labor enterprises and institutions.

The participants in the courses are selected by the trade unions, cooperatives, and government ministries dealing with development, labor, and cooperation. They include senior trade union officials; cooperative institution and ministry officials; leaders, activists, and organizers in specific fields; and teaching staffs of universities and institutes of higher learning.

The Afro-Asian Institute for Cooperative and Labour studies (AAI) provides the bulk of the budget. Additional funds come from scholarships offered by trade unions in the United States, Great Britain, and Switzerland, and international trade secretariats and organizations, including the Common Market, U.N. Development Program, and the government of Israel, which offers travel expenses not covered by AAI. Generally there are more candidates for these courses than there are places. From time to time governments, mainly in countries that are not aware of the real nature of the institute, forbid particpation in AAI courses. One Israeli ambassador, inquiring whether his country of accreditation would be interested in sending students to one of these courses, received a very sharp reaction. He was informed that "trade unions" was considered a dirty term, and "cooperation" on the border.

To meet the growing demand for its courses, in 1964 the AAI started to send staff members abroad to conduct concentrated local seminars. This also provided the opportunity to meet and observe former students, to conduct evaluation surveys, and to provide a simple refresher course where indicated.

In June 1970 the Regional Asian Seminar was held in Seoul, Korea. It was organized by the Freidrich Ebert Foundation in conjunction with AAI, and its proceedings were published.

The opening lectures of the seminars reflected the main fields of interest, expertise, and approach of the speakers. The German participants discussed social demands in a modern society, economic development and social justice, and trade unions and their role in society. Israelis concentrated on specifics in the developing countries: the comprehensive character of development problems in Asia and the role of cooperation and labor, cooperative planning in developing countries, and various aspects of cooperation activity of trade unions in developing countries.

In the lecture by Akiva Eger, principal of the AAI, emphasis was on the primary need to train adequate personnel for carrying out development in the developing countries. The shortage of such personnel impairs the effectiveness of such projects and was the chief reason for the failure of the First Development Decade (1961-70). Training of manpower—the training of managers and qualified labor—is a top priority for development."[1]

In a developing country there is need for an integrated approach to cooperation and to trade unionism. The poorest part of society is the small peasants; they are the most underprivileged and not the wage earners.[2] Consequently developing countries should promote the idea of a common approach to urban and rural workers and a joint trade union movement.

Only an integrated approach, combining all aspects of development, can assure progress. A recurrent problem is the need to close the gap between rural and urban society and to build "a bridge between the mainly cooperative rural movement, making the cooperative and the trade union movements two arms of the same body to embrace the problems of national development."[3]

In Seoul, Akiva Eger presented the quintessence of the Israeli approach to development. He gave the case for mobilization of trade unionism and cooperativism for national development in developing countries. Another Israeli lecturer, Richie Zavidov, provided an additional element of Israeli doctrine by stressing the need for planning realistically and thus avoiding, or at least narrowing, the gap between planning and implementation.[4] A third Israeli, Yair Levi, described and analyzed practical instances of interrelation between trade unions and cooperatives in developing countries.[5]

The report of the study groups of the Seoul seminar bears witness of the remarkable way in which the leading idea of the course was accepted, although it was presented with caution. It describes the need for a coordinated movement by trade unions and cooperatives—despite the fact that history has shown that the two movements are difficult to merge. The suggested areas for joint action are cooperatives in services, industry, and housing. Because of the difficulty in merging these two movements, the study group recommended the creation of a coordinating council.

In its bulletin the AAI publishes a section devoted to letters from former students. Sometimes they evidence concrete application of the ideas inculcated by AAI. A participant from Kenya wrote: "I have become the initiator of several projects hanging around my area. This being a small village, I organize study groups as well as study circles. I lecture on cooperation and social activities, and through these activities we are gradually improving."[6]

The Centre for Cooperation and Labour Studies for Latin America has been established on lines similar, but not identical, to those of the AAI. The chief difference is that the Centre does not offer the same courses each year. Subjects vary from time to time, depending on the joint recommendations of the Latin American countries and the Organization of American States. In the period from 1962 to 1972 the Centre conducted 39 courses in Israel and a similar number in Latin America, with the participation of some 2,000 students.

These courses fell into two categories:

1.   Courses dealing with problems of cooperation and trade unionism, where the center used its own literature and its own organization and followed its own "doctrine." Subjects included agrarian cooperation, auditing of agricultural cooperatives, trade unions and cooperation, employment and labor exchanges, and cooperative marketing of agricultural products.[7]

2.   Courses conducted by the Centre with the joint planning of the Organiza-

tion of American States, the Centre serving as an "executive agency." These included health services in rural zones, popular housing, and financing of urban development.

TRANSPORTATION

A long-term project in service cooperation is one in Peru. Israel has been advising the National Institute for Cooperatives since the early 1960s. Since 1965 the Institute has sought Israeli assistance in urban services and the organization of transport cooperation. Members of *Egged*, Israel's principal transport cooperative, served as experts for a protracted period. Surveys were conducted, studies were made, and finally a master plan for interurban transportation was presented and accepted. The experts held courses in this field and students from other Latin American countries participated. The project which was begun on a bilateral basis, in its later stages was partly adopted by the International Labour Organization and Organization of American States. After its successful development several countries expressed a keen interest in advice on the organization of transport cooperatives.

BANKS

What at one time might have seemed a contradiction in terms—assistance by the workers' organizations in one country to a banking operation in another—turned out to be a very interesting, far-reaching and successful project. In 1963 the labor ministers of Latin America, at a meeting in Bogotá, recommended that workers' banks be set up. Since 1968 Israelis have been assisting in the implementation of this recommendation. As of 1972 workers' banks had been established in Puerto Rico, Guatemala, Honduras, Venezuela, and Trinidad. Eight other countries in Latin America have had similar projects under consideration. The newly established banks have been using the experience and general principles of organization of the Bank Hapoalim—the Workers' Bank of Israel.

The main objective of these banks, according to Israeli advisors, is to bring about active participation of workers in the developmental process of their countries. Therefore the banks are owned jointly by the workers, the unions, the cooperatives, and the respective government. They serve not only as instruments for assuring a fair rate of return for money but also as institutions for savings and for the building up of the social infrastructure in housing and education.

The Israeli experts provided advice on the appointment of resident advisors, the preparation of laws and statutes for banks, the periodic supervisory visits, and the organization of seminars. The subject matter of these seminars included bank organization, bank accounting, savings schemes, and development projects.

The general lines of assistance provided by the Bank Hapoalim to Latin American banks were established in an agreement by the Fritz Naphtali Foundation with the Organization of American States and the Inter-American Development Bank. The Bank Hapoalim and the Bank Für Gemeinwirtschaft maintain close contact with the new banks in order to assist in their growth and development along the lines of their original objectives. The project is also closely watched and assisted by the Social Affairs Department of the Organization of American States and the Inter-American Development Bank.

The fact that Israeli assistance is sought outside agriculture—in transportation and even banking—reflects the diversified needs in developing countries. However, the basic characteristics remain the same—the preoccupation of developing countries with involving the most levels of the population possible in the process of national development, and the continuing interest in drawing on the Israeli experience and expertise to achieve this end. This is due largely to the unique roles played in Israel's history by the labor movement, the cooperatives, the trade unions, and the wide spectrum of other Histadrut functions, all of which since their beginnings have believed in and practiced broad identification of their own objectives with the wide national targets.

NOTES

1.   Akiva Eger, "The Comprehensive Character of Development Problems in Asia and the Role of Cooperation and Labour," in Klaus Pretzer and Hans Dietrich Bollow, eds., *Trade Unions and Cooperatives in the Development of Asia, Regional Asian Seminar, 1970, Seoul, Republic of Korea* (Bonn: Friedrich Ebert Stiftung, International Department, 1971), p. 61.

2.   Ibid, p. 70.

3.   Ibid, p. 71.

4.   R. Zavidov, "Cooperative Planning in Developing Countries," in Pretzer and Bollow, eds., *Trade Unions and Cooperatives* . . . , p.75.

5.   Y. Levi, "Various Aspects of the Cooperative Activity of Trade Unions in Developing Countries," in Pretzer and Bollow, eds., *Trade Unions and Cooperatives* . . . , p. 141.

6.   *The Afro-Asian Institute Bulletin*, no. 8, December 1966, p. 19.

7.   See Ministry for Foreign Affairs, International Cooperation Division, *Courses in Israel, 1970-73* (Jerusalem: the Ministry, 1970), pp. 35-45.

The development of human resources is among the chief objectives of practically all development programs. In a broad sense this objective encompasses two similar but not identical concepts—education and training. Education aims at the general advancement of the personality and the intellectual capacity of the individual. Training, more limited in scope, imparts specific skills and practical information. A wise man once defined education as that which is left to us after we forget what we have learned. Training, on the other hand, is what we have learned and retained so that we can perform a specific function.

Certainly there is a relationship between both, and those who are better educated are usually easier to train in various skills. There always remains, however, the dilemma of priorities. In times of emergency, such as war, it has always been possible to conduct training without injecting those elements of general knowledge not directly related to the specific task to be performed.

Mutatis mutandis, however, this distinction is to a great degree the basis for discussions concerning the provision of pure science as opposed to applied science. While many important discoveries and inventions resulted from the application of pure science, in developing countries the question of practical priorities looms large. Research institutes occasionally become involved in theoretical problems far removed from the needs of local society. In other cases such institutions are conducting studies of vital importance but lack the means to impart their findings quickly and efficiently to an interested public. There are cases where excellent results are achieved in developing methods of increasing crop yields while the surrounding farmers do not know of or profit from these discoveries for many years. Both cases reflect the regrettable phenomenon of estrangement between the scientist, as such, and society at large—mainly at the grass roots level, in agriculture, industry, or services. Another manifestation of this estrangement is the trend of many scholars to get away from the production line and into the ivory tower atmosphere of the research institute or into public administration.

Israeli experts emphasize the social responsibility of scientists particularly in young countries. Since scientists have benefited from society because of their prolonged years of education, they are under an obligation to repay this debt to society by tackling problem-oriented issues.

There are some interesting examples to be garnered from Israel's own experience. The notable advancement of agriculture is due in large part to the constant communication between scientists, producers, and extension officers. Of significant interest are the joint planning committees, presided over by the Planning Department of the Ministry of Agriculture. Their function is to establish both long- and short-range targets. Representatives of the producers present their needs and make forecasts according to market development. Scientists project prospects and limitations from their point of view, and extension officers prepare detailed action plans for the implementation of contemplated changes. Thus it has been possible to prepare for the production and marketing of new products and the modification of old ones.

Another development in Israel's history brings useful conclusions. Some years ago the upcoming generation of physicians indicated a growing unwillingness to move to development areas. Benefits of various kinds and improvement in salary scales did not provide sufficient incentive for them to leave metropolitan areas. After a vast amount of questioning it was established that young doctors were especially keen on being close to research facilities. Subsequently, by converting a number of hospitals into de facto medical schools, it was possible to entice medical students into moving. Thus hospitals were able to fulfill the triple functions of service, teaching, and research.

Possibly this integrated approach presages optimal development not only in higher education but in the educational system as a whole. A report commissioned by the Organization for Economic Cooperation and Development indicates the advantages of combining pragmatic tasks performed by young students with theoretical learning.[1] "This can be achieved by giving them responsibility for tasks which affect the welfare of their fellow humans. It is by rendering contributions to the adult community and by being treated as adults that they will learn adult roles."[2] In this atmosphere young people are induced to study through practical work. In the case of the medical students the combination of the opportunity for study and research served as an inducement to work in remote areas. In each case the integration of differing functions seems to produce fertile effects.

Most assistance projects carried out with Israeli participation in the fields of science, research, and higher education combine several functions. A case in point is the microbiology project at the Haile Selassie I University of Addis Ababa. Contact between Israeli scientists and universities and those of Addis Ababa have been maintained for many years. A number of Israelis served on the faculty of the Ethiopian university.

The Ethiopian-Israeli Joint Microbiology Program started during the academic year 1970-71 and was planned for five years. It was conceived as a tripartite project in which the participants are the Haile Selassie I University of Addis Ababa, the

Hebrew University, and the Division of International Cooperation of the Ministry for Foreign Affairs of Israel. The costs of the project are borne by the three partners.

The aim of this project is to create an independent, full-fledged department of microbiology staffed by Ethiopian teachers at the end of the five-year period. In addition, a number of students will be taught general biology, medicine, and pharmacy, and will receive accreditation. The studies to be stressed are microbiology, immunology, and virology. Tuition is provided for some students in sanitation microbiology and industrial fermentation.

Interest in the course has been growing steadily, and the number of students exceeds the capacity originally planned. During the first year there were 33 students; during the second, 50, and in the third, 60. Among many interesting developments has been the transfer of some teaching activities to a hospital in order to bring about better integration with further clinical studies.

Teaching is conducted by a substantial number of Israelis for periods of limited duration. Although this method has the advantage of ensuring top specialists for each subject, there was a feeling among the Ethiopian university teachers that a longer stay by the Israelis would enable them to achieve better integration on the campus.

Particular stress is placed on the preparation of future teachers for the department. Every report by the directors of the project carries a detailed proposal for the staffing of the department together with the names of candidates and their specialization, from the Hebrew University in Jerusalem or elsewhere.

The multiplier effect of this project was recently manifested when UNESCO requested an Israeli from the teaching staff of the project to serve as the international organizer for a training course in microbiology to be held at Addis Ababa in 1973 or 1974, following a recommendation by an International Cell Research Organization UNESCO panel held in São Paulo in July 1972.

SYMPOSIA WITH THE OAS

Since 1970, scientific symposia have been held jointly with several Latin American countries and in coordination with the Organization of American States. Those in Venezuela and in Argentina dealt with plant genetics and hydrology. The one in 1973 is planned to deal with water contamination.

Water

Following previous contacts with governments and regional organizations, in 1971 a mission made up of the heads of research institutes in Israel visited Brazil, Argentina, Chile, Peru, and Mexico to present a plan for creating a regional institute for research on arid zones. The report of the mission suggests using existing institutes to create teams of scientists who, with their Israeli counterparts, could advance research and training in problems concerning hydrology, irrigation, optimal use of water, and physiology of plants and animals in arid zones. In view of the large arid areas in the countries mentioned, it is natural that the project aroused considerable interest. Nevertheless, as with any regional project, the gestation period is long and this is still in the initial stages of exploration.

An agreement signed in 1972 between the Council for Science and Technology of Mexico and the National Council for Research and Development of Israel (an official entity in the prime minister's office) envisages an exchange of teachers and students and joint research projects, mainly in agriculture, genetics, hydrology, ecology, and food technology. An agreement signed the same year with Chile concentrates on integral development of arid and semiarid zones. In the discussions of both agreements the Israeli delegation included members of the Division for International Cooperation and of the International Agricultural Cooperation Centre, to ensure as far as possible the integration of ongoing cooperation field projects in new research programs.

Energy

Some years ago much hope was placed in the rapid development of the use of solar energy. Apart from its application in installing water heaters in countries having a sufficient number of sunny days per annum, the hopes did not materialize as anticipated. The much-desired small-scale solar turbine has not advanced from its experimental stage.

In 1972 discussions were in progress on a number of joint projects in food and plant radiation and the use of isotopes in hydrological studies. Most of the projects in the use of atomic energy for peaceful purposes were conducted in Brazil.

Agriculture

A number of successful joint scientific ventures took place in agricultural research. From 1969 on, a new allocation was made in the operational budget of the International Agricultural Cooperation Centre for research on the most urgent problems affecting some of the current projects. The work is being conducted by members of research institutions in Israel in close cooperation with parallel institutions in the countries concerned and with the regional institutes. Communications between scientists and field experts took place between Israel and Asia, Africa, and Latin America.

Practical results achieved during three years of research included improvement of quantity of yields, length of season, or better quality in the production of tomatoes, onions, potatoes, corn, and cotton in Asia; of peanuts in Latin America and Africa; and of sorghum in Asia and in Africa. The result of production of a specific hybrid variety of sorghum in Cambodia was spectacular. Three crops were grown in one year, each crop producing 15 tons per hectare, compared with an average crop of 3 tons per hectare. The prospects for a breakthrough, and new horizons for economic and agricultural planning are optimistic; but they certainly are not as high as those achieved experimentally. Unless the new variety is introduced on a wider scale, any firm conclusions are premature.

SCIENTIFIC PROGRAMS

In trying to assess the projects conducted in Israel, it seems that the most ambitious were the courses for doctors and agricultural engineers, initiated during the early 1960s and discontinued toward the end of the same decade.

The motives for this venture were natural and obvious. The courses were planned for the emerging countries of Africa, and only during the later stages was it decided to make them available to countries of the Mediterranean area and of Asia as well.

The decision to start these projects was brought on by an awareness of the tremendous shortage of such personnel in the countries in question. For example, African countries have the lowest ratio of doctors for their populations in the world. "It has been estimated [in 1968] that Africa alone needs more than 80,000 doctors in order to achieve the modest ratio of one physician for every 10,000 inhabitants. That would necessitate the training of about 13,000 doctors during the next ten years."[3]

Against this tremendous need the contribution of Israel is modest. Between 1961 and 1964, 75 students from 12 countries were admitted for a 6-year course and a seventh year for internship. Of these, 11 students dropped out, chiefly because of academic failure; 64 completed their studies, and some went on for higher degrees.

In evaluating their studies a large majority of the students expressed satisfaction with the choice of school, the curriculum, and the results. Many showed interest in joining teaching staffs or research groups in developing countries.[4] The chief complaint leveled by these students was the lack of close personal relations with their Israeli colleagues. This aspect is difficult to judge, because it has been suggested that an inherent weakness in the Israeli student is the lack of interest in those things which do not concern him directly.[5]

In summing up, the evaluation study concludes: "It is yet premature to make a complete and objective evaluation of the success of the course. Indications at present suggest that it has succeeded in training good physicians and a considerable portion of these will go into training or research."[6]

In spite of the overall success of the medical courses, it was decided to discontinue them. The question of language—the need for students to learn Hebrew in order to attend those classes not held in English—although influencing this decision, was only a secondary consideration. The chief reason was the change that took place in the developing countries themselves. In many countries and regions medical schools were established. It became part of the accepted doctrine of development to give precedence to national or regional courses for undergraduates, rather than courses in other areas. It not only was a question of economy; it was believed that basic training should take place in conditions as near as possible to those prevailing in the student's own surroundings.

Perhaps another closely related reason should be mentioned. Undergraduate studies are, by their nature, prolonged and usually commence at the end of the students' adolescence. A young man who leaves his country at the age of 18 returns, after completion of studies and internship, at the age of 25, a completely different person. Not only does he face a different milieu, but those who receive him face a different man. As a consequence there is need for a twofold confrontation and adaptation that complicates an already complex situation.

The decision to discontinue undergraduate studies was accompanied by a belief that they should be replaced by postgraduate training. The students would be mature, integrated into their society, and performing professional duties in their own countries. Courses would be shorter and problems of social adaptation would be less intense. Particular attention would be given to the training of teachers.

In 1968, when undergraduate studies were discontinued, the Hebrew University Hadassah Medical School (HUHMS) started to prepare a two-year course for teachers in medical schools in developing countries. In this project, as in the previous one, the World Health Organization (WHO) offered scholarships to suitable candidates in interested countries.

Undergraduate courses in agricultural engineering were held at the Technion, Israel Institute of Technology. During 1963-66 about 100 students were admitted to courses leading to a B.Sc. degree that included the basic elements for modern agriculture and rural engineering, with special emphasis on water, irrigation, and tropical agriculture. These courses were discontinued for similar reasons. Most of the almost 70 graduates integrated well in their countries, in both executive and teaching functions. Seven continued postgraduate studies, and one is working on his Ph.D. dissertation. In a number of countries, students faced difficulties because degrees in agricultural engineering were unknown. The problems, however, were solved quickly; and many countries have introduced this discipline following the Israeli example.

At the present time postgraduate or specialized studies for students from developing countries are being conducted by Israeli institutions—both academic and research—in underground water, agricultural meteorology, food technology, and irrigation, as well as medicine and agriculture.

Academic training projects are problem-oriented and in areas where Israel has sufficient expertise. The multiplier effect is the guideline, and training of teachers is considered of greater importance than training of doers. In the various disciplines special attention is paid to those of broad social application and impact. In the field of medicine, for example, a continuing course, already repeated several times, is the two-year study leading to a diploma in public health. The director of the course arrived in Israel some time ago to introduce the discipline of public health under the aegis of the WHO, at a time when Israel was the recipient. This alone may be cited as a multiplier effect of technical assistance.

Evolution in a similar vein was provided in an important branch of medicine in which Israel is active. Since 1959, when the chief of the Ophthalmology

Department of HUMS was invited to Liberia to direct a survey for the treatment of the blind and to plan an education program for them, Israel has been active in many African countries in a number of different ways. Some four to six Israeli eye specialists have been constantly attached to hospitals for up to two years. Nurses have been trained in eye problems both in Israel and abroad. African physicians have studied ophthalmology at the Hebrew University. A number of research projects have been initiated, mainly with the participation of doctors with experience in Africa.

It is not easy to recruit suitable young candidates in the building of their careers for service abroad. Professor Isaac Michaelson, chief of the Ophthalmology Department of HUMS, succeeded, however, in filling the vacancies for 13 years. In addition to creating interest and a feeling of duty among his students, both vital for service abroad, Professor Michaelson established a new unwritten rule: service in Africa was to be a precondition for admission to his department in nearly every case, and this was certainly true for any type of distinction or promotion.

In 1972 Michaelson initiated an international seminar to stress the need for concentrating on the preservation of sight and the prevention of blindness. Instead of looking for a cure, the doctor spreads necessary information for the prevention of blindness. It follows the now accepted belief that preventive medicine should be accorded not less attention than curative.

Professor Michaelson's recent step into the adventure of ideas revolves about the founding of a new center for the preservation of sight. It will relate to clinical and research activities in existing opthalmological establishments in Israel and Africa; provide preventive solutions through legislation, teaching, public information, and education; and serve as a link with the Israel National Committee for the Prevention of Blindness and similar committees abroad.

Foreign trainees in Israel have been impressed by the practical, problem-oriented approach characterizing local studies, including medicine. They have also indicated that the rich experience of their teachers and tutors in international cooperation with developing countries facilitated the adaptation of studies to their needs.

Medical projects abroad were conducted chiefly in Africa. One of particular interest was the School for Medical Assistants in Malawi. For many years Israeli experts participated in this program that provided medical assistants in rural areas, where the shortage of doctors is the most acute.

A general look at Israel's scientific policy was presented during the Israeli-Latin American Symposium on Science Policy and Organization of Research in 1970.[7] The symposium was organized jointly by the Organization of American States and by the National Council for Research and Development of Israel. The Latin Americans were particularly interested in examining Israeli experience because of the growing awareness of the need to provide new orientation for the academic and scientific institutions in Latin America.

The salient feature of the Israeli presentation was the interchange between science, research, and higher education and production, industry, agriculture, and services, both in the private and in the national sectors. This was the main theme of the Rehovot Movement, expressed in a series of Rehovot conferences. In 1960 the first of these conferences was convened by Abba Eban, at that time president of the Weizmann Institute of Science in Rehovot. The theme of that conference was the role of science in the advancement of new states. There were 120 delegates from some 40 countries in attendance. They were made up of two groups—the leaders of new nations and prominent scientists from all over the world.

Conferences meeting since 1963 on a biennial basis have dealt with comprehensive planning of agriculture, monetary and fiscal problems, education, and urbanization. The 1973 conference will examine noneconomic factors of national growth.

Characteristic of the Rehovot conferences was the continuing confrontation of men of action, national leaders—the doers—with men of science and research—the thinkers. It is a new expression of the Platonic preoccupation with relations between kings and philosophers. The Rehovot formula, however, appears to be not a replacement of kings by philosophers but, rather, their confrontation and interaction.

NOTES

1.   Torsten Husén, *Social Background and Educational Career* (Paris: Organization for Economic Cooperation and Development, 1972), as reviewed in the *OECD Observer*, no. 60, October 1972, pp. 9-12.

2.   Ibid., p. 12.

3.   Quoted in Olusegan Fayami, *Evaluation of the Course for Medical Students from Developing Countries* (Jerusalem: HUHMS, 1968), p. 1.

4.   Ibid., p. 26.

5.   Ibid., p. 33.

6.   Ibid., p. 40.

7.   Eliezer Tal and Yaron Ezrachi, eds., *Science Policy and Development—The Case of Israel* (New York: Gordon and Breach, 1972).

The chairman of the Development Assistance Committee of the Organization for Economic Cooperation and Development (OECD) leveled severe criticism at one aspect of education assistance projects:

> Given the volume of money and manpower now being devoted to education, its key potential role in creating modern states able to meet their citizens' needs, and the long lag between starting to train teachers in new curricula and the graduation into society of youth whose education has all been of [a] modern and relevant type, it is a cause for great concern that more effort is not being spent on finding out what should be done instead of busily offering more and more of the same out-of-date or out-of-context types of education.[1]

The situation in technical assistance in general is not much better. Perhaps the entire development community—at both the receiving and the giving ends—should make greater efforts to determine whether what is being done represents the optimal meeting point between the needs of the recipient and the capabilities and potential of the donor. Israel's record, in this respect at least, is no better than most.

In spite of its recognized awareness of the need for more systematic evaluation of the existing projects and of the optimal conditions for new ones, only a few beginnings have actually been made to establish satisfactory procedures and mechanisms for such an evaluation. This defect would appear to reflect a characteristic feature of the Israeli way of life: concentration on doing and performing, without paying enough attention to analyzing and reflecting.

Out of Israel's rich experience gathered by its diplomatic personnel and technical aides abroad, as well as from work at home with trainees from many lands, several ex post facto conclusions can be drawn. The conclusions are far from being firm, and in some instances they might be refuted by Israeli technicians. Essentially they conform with today's generally accepted norms, but at the same time they reflect to a great degree many of Israel's national characteristics.

The following study is concerned basically with four factors: project selection, experts, trainees, and assistance between and among developing countries.

It is commonly accepted that the most decisive element in any assistance program is identification of projects. Because needs always exceed available resources, special attention must be given to selecting the best possible projects. The Agency for International Development's criteria of project evaluation, aimed at establishing a project's maximum significance, effectiveness, and efficiency, indicate the most desirable features of any development project.[2] Ideally these criteria must bear their weight even during the exploratory stages of project identification.

Israel's practice in this respect has been to attempt a speedy decision—from within a few weeks, say, up to two months. By that time, it is reasoned, an interested country should be able to ascertain whether a request for an assistance project can be met. When the answer is yes, professional individuals or teams from the sector in which the project is requested, occasionally accompanied by a member of the Division for International Cooperation, visit the country, usually for two or three weeks, to explore the details of the request and discuss the possibilities and limits of Israel's participation. Their findings are examined in Jerusalem and are included in a more or less detailed report. If everything is clear and agreed upon, an assistance project might start within six months of an initial request.

As a rule Israeli advisors prefer to begin with a small, limited project and, as its potential and practicality are established, work it into a larger project. The earlier project is sometimes described as a "pioneer project," one of a more advanced nature than a "pilot project," which does not have a built-in potential for multiplication. More than one sympathetic outside observer, recognizing the value of a sound in-depth project, has simultaneously criticized Israelis for the limited dimensions of projects recommended by them. Israel's response to this criticism has been that the central challenge of development programs lies in the preparation and availability of suitable local manpower. It has since also pointed out that the tremendous difficulties and problems involved require much more effort to overcome than anyone not directly involved in meeting the challenge could hope to know. Israel points out, too, that in the initial stages the potential of high-level technicians and local leaders able to implement desired projects is limited and that the size of a planned project must take into account the very tangible problem of the potential availability of manpower.

Perhaps the fact that in the majority of cases Israelis are involved in concrete field projects makes them more acutely aware of the actual difficulties of implementation, especially those related to problems of manpower. Nevertheless, discussions have been held with the aim of establishing methods of planning projects on a larger scale. Among these methods would certainly be intensification of the elements of training and the creation of a suitable personnel cadre on different levels. This trend coincides nicely with the recently evolved practice that obtains in large assistance projects, among them those established by the International Bank for Reconstruction and Development or the Inter-American Development Bank: to establish in each project a specific budget for technical assistance explicitly related to the project. Several Israel-assisted projects in conjunction with the Inter-American Development Bank and the Organization of American States are partly financed by such budgets. They embrace a variety of projects and functions, including experimentation farms, local training courses, specialization in Israel itself for more highly trained employees, and preparation of professional reports on such subjects as cooperative marketing and directed credit.

Given a choice, Israelis prefer a field project during the early stages rather than an advisory position at headquarters. This organic approach, engendered by grass roots experience, enables them to obtain an immediate gauge of desired changes and observe their actual mechanics. If an unsuitable element is detected in this process, it can easily be revised precisely because the project is limited and the discovery of its flaws feasible at an early stage. The experience thus obtained on a small scale can then be multiplied and the necessary manpower trained in the interim.

When an *in situ* project has been well established, there is a need for access to the policy-making body at headquarters. Such access can sometimes be provided by a close working relationship between a chief project advisor and the respective headquarters official. In other cases a project advisor can get an official appointment as an advisor at headquarters or a special advisor may be named. In any event, to achieve real support for the new "doctrine" as represented by a specific project, it is necessary to obtain support from the relevant central policy-making authority. Otherwise the project will not get off the ground and develop into a national or regional plan transcending local importance.

The most successful development occurs when a project is institutionalized after general acceptance, either as an adapted part of an existing institution or as a new institution, or even as an entity created by law. The ideal modality of an organic multistage development project, therefore, would be a small experimental field project, growing into a larger pilot project with a multiplier effect, followed by the appointment of an advisor in a central authority and the completion of the process by an institution-building law. The case of supervised credit in agriculture in Venezuela (see Chapter 4), which started with some tens of families and evolved by 1970 into a project of almost 20,000 families and the formation of the training institute CIARA, serves as an illustration of a multistage process of a development project. In the Service Civique of the Ivory Coast, the local government requested that an Israeli advisor at headquarters work concurrently with field experts from the beginning of a project because it wanted to ensure permanent communication and support between headquarters and the field.

Israel's experience on the whole, then, has been satisfactory when assisting in project identification and implementation. What still needs elaboration is joint evaluation and jointly accepted programs of phasing out. Since the decision-making process has as a rule been very speedy, not enough attention has been paid to elements of joint review and evaluation. Many assistance projects remain open-ended operations, and sometimes the wish of Israelis to reduce the role of their own advisors and to accelerate the complete handover to local personnel is not easily understood. An intermediate measure has been a joint, annual high-level meeting to review and evaluate both past performance and future plans. New programs, such as the microbiology project in Ethiopia (see Chapter 8), specify the length of time the project will last. In a technical type of project, naturally, the timetable can more easily be ascertained than, for example, in a youth program or an agricultural project in which problems are more complex and less predictable. There is nevertheless a growing awareness of the need to include a specific timetable for every new project in every new sector. This element, as well as others, should be included in the planning stage—not because there is a high degree of probability that the planned target will be achieved exactly (a rare achievement) but, rather, because timetables are necessary and useful as an indicative checklist of considerations that should be jointly understood by assisting and assisted nations in each development project, both in the selection and planning stages and in the subsequent implementation and evaluation.

In Israel's practice there has never been a sharp distinction between advisors and operational experts, between experts attached to officials in a local administrative hierarchy solely in an advisory capacity and experts performing established functions in that hierarchy. In some cases they hold a clearly defined responsibility for the former, in others for the latter; often their functions combine aspects of both. This is, of course, a de facto situation not always defined in a formal job description. Perhaps this state of affairs explains their advisors' high degree of personal involvement in and identification with the projects. In some instances this' situation has resulted in conflicts with the local hierarchy, creating "short circuits" —Israeli experts bypassing proper channels to achieve pragmatic, quick solutions to urgent problems, often addressing themselves to higher echelons of the administration.

Experts on agriculture, even when invited to fulfill a well-defined assignment of a limited nature, are often requested by their local counterparts to offer advice beyond their specifically sought competence. They are implicitly expected to be general interlocutors and advisors on matters of development at large, able to present and interpret Israel's own experience in fields of development under consideration. Among the successful agricultural team leaders in special demand have been comprehensive planners with experience in colonization and economic planning, experts able to offer a comprehensive view of problems and solutions.

With the passage of time it has become increasingly difficult to find suitable candidates for service abroad because the availability of experts has decreased and because the expectations and demands of receiving nations have increased. Some years ago, sound practical experience in a *kibbutz* or *moshav*, embodied in a suitable personality, qualified a candidate for service abroad. Now receiving countries often also require a formal university degree. One reason for this phenomenon is that Israeli counterparts in receiving countries are themselves university graduates who expect foreign experts to possess at least a comparable formal education. Experience has demonstrated, however, that often the most successful experts are those with the greatest practical experience in the field, not necessarily those with university degrees. The ideal candidate, admittedly, would be a member of a *kibbutz* or *moshav* with university-level education in agriculture, but such a candidate is a rare species in Israeli projects because their supply is limited.

The growing shortage of highly qualified experts has forced Israel to establish a system of aid combining teams of a few highly qualified experts serving as team leaders and a number of field experts, usually with rich practical experience, supported by short-term specialists. For example, El Sisal, a project in the Dominican Republic for the settling in a rural center of some 500 agricultural families and an additional 100 families, is staffed by two permanent Israeli advisors. In 1971 and 1972 it was supported by short-term assignments of experts in physical planning, irrigation, fishery, and horticulture. In the same period a project in Zambia was supported by experts in marketing, agricultural planning, physical planning, and field crops. Both projects are already in advanced stages of implementation. During the first years, of course, the support of short-term experts is more intensive.

One of the techniques used to achieve a more regular supply of experts is the assurance of institutional support. A project in Ethiopia is a case in point. Instead of trying to persuade the Department of Microbiology of Hebrew University to release some of its members for service in Ethiopia, the Division for International Cooperation requested that the department deal with the project in its entirety. Given this arrangement, the fact that department members were leaving on tours of duty in the field was viewed not as a case of depleting the faculty but as an extension of one of its branches into a new area of particular interest and challenge. This way of farming out projects to institutions proved practical in two other cases of medical assistance—one in Kenya and one in Rwanda. In a symposium on international cooperation held in Jerusalem in 1969 by leaders in Israel medicine, a recommendation was carried to go for a combined venture—not between hospitals or universities as such but among departments of both. It would appear that only such direct links among operational units over a prolonged period can assure continuing interest and support on the part of the donor institution.

Continual efforts are being made to improve procedures and methods of preparing experts for their posts abroad. Whenever possible, prolonged courses in languages, specific professional preparation, and general knowledge of developing nations are conducted for experts in agriculture and youth activities. More difficult is the training of personnel in other fields, in which the number of experts is small. Particular emphasis has been placed in recent years on training in basic subjects, such as applied pedagogy and visual aids, and on training in general subjects of relevance to developing countries, all with the awareness that quite often in purely professional fields, ability to communicate and generate enthusiasm and involvement among local personnel is more important than becoming fully "up-to-date."

Apart from formal training courses, continuous attention is being paid to individual training and preparation. All experts, and especially heads of projects, are briefed by their professional institutions, by members of the Division for International Cooperation, and by area officers. Whenever possible, a special program of visits to relevant places and institutions is arranged.

The importance of training experts' wives has been widely recognized. A study group associated with the Hebrew University's Department of African Studies points clearly to a correlation between the training of experts' wives and the experts' own success in performing their duties.[3] Several attempts have been made to enable wives with relevant knowledge to participate actively and continuously in some areas of developmental programs. Difficulties in getting women for service abroad is being experienced mainly in the field of community development, as indicated in Chapter 6. In other fields a number of women experts have participated successfully since the beginning of cooperation programs. In the last few years women experts have served in medicine, vocational training, and scientific research in agriculture and medicine.

Given the shortage of experts, Israelis have tried to employ "veteran experts," those with previous experience abroad. As a rule it is assumed that an expert should stay in one country from three to five years before returning home. After spending several years abroad and becoming conversant with professional and general currents and changes, the expert would be encouraged to go abroad again, but usually not to the same country. Attempts are now being made to establish more lasting contacts with past experts, according to countries in which they have specialized, by having them perform such vital functions as serving as hosts in Israel to trainees from countries in which they once worked, serving as members of selection committees or as tutors to aspiring experts, going abroad as short-term consultants, or possibly serving a second tour of duty. Because of the rather large number of veteran experts, however, it has proved difficult to find a viable, interesting way of maintaining productive contact with them.

Means of achieving or advancing this objective have yet to be found, the central question remaining whether veteran experts should be organized on a purely professional basis, not taking into account the country of their service. The need to establish a satisfactory means of keeping in touch with them, however, remains one of the most serious challenges facing Israel in this realm. Experts themselves have often voiced their disappointment over this deficient communication. When a suitable solution is found to the problem, these veteran experts will become valuable promoters in Israel of wide support for increased programs of international cooperation, an action needed in view of several Israeli setbacks in 1972 in relations with some of the developing countries in Africa.

With regard to the question of the relative advantages and disadvantages of bringing trainees to Israel vis-à-vis local training programs, some conclusions have been drawn. Obviously the cost of bringing people to Israel or to any donor country is greater than that of training them at home. In the case of Israel, however, cost must defer to expertise, for training in Israel simply cannot be matched by training in recipient countries for a very obvious reason: An integral part of Israel's assistance program is Israel's own on-scene development and performance, which must be considered and examined at close hand, quite apart from and beyond purely professional, theoretical, and technical skills taught or information communicated. Observing and evaluating development in action—in the field—and the results of specific accelerated, successful development in the concrete can only be experienced in Israel. The country serves as a training ground; its very growth and development, and even its problems and difficulties, are a living example of its teaching and assistance. Furthermore, the advantage of training in still-developing Israel as opposed to training in a more completely established nation is one of both degree and time dimension. In an established developed country a trainee from a developing country might well experience a feeling of a deep, unbridgeable distance between the situation in his own and in his host-donor country. In Israel, on the other hand, he can hear from his tutors their own personal histories of progress, experimentation, and transformation. He is likely to leave Israel not only equipped with new techniques but also inspired by faith that what has been achieved in this small land can be achieved in his own country in his own lifetime.

Most of the courses held in Israel contain a sizable element of practical work and observation. Only 50 percent or less of teaching time is spent in classes. Trainees in agriculture are attached to members of cooperative villages for weeks and are familiarized with the complete machinery and procedure of their work in the field, in the courtyard, and at home. The kindergarten teachers spend entire days in kindergartens with Israeli teachers, and students in the postgraduate course in hydrology participate in long field trips and actual exploration for underground water resources.

Apart from the longer courses (mainly postgraduate) already referred to, in addition to individual studies, the majority of trainees come to Israel for courses of some three to four months' duration. The courses combine theoretical studies with practical work and experimentation. Special emphasis is placed on observations of concrete solutions evolved in Israel. A major element of the courses, therefore, consists of numerous, intensive tours and visits to relevant institutions and discussions with Israeli officials concerning the optimal approach to the subject matter and an examination of case studies.

An indispensable part of any course is the will to inculcate the belief that trainees can be self-generating in acquiring a conviction of their own power and enthusiasm and that as a consequence they can apply their creative change of attitude to practical problems when they return home. This is the major precondition of achieving meaningful results on the way to modernization and development. This rather imponderable, even mystical pioneering spirit of dedication to altruistic causes, as idealistic as it might seem to modern skeptics, is in fact the most realistic, most vital goal sought by trainees in Israeli programs. For without faith in one's own practical power to change man's environment for the better, even on a small scale, that change cannot occur.

The majority of visitors to Israel have been trained by the Department of Foreign Taining in the Ministry of Agriculture. Between 1960 and 1972 some 4,500 trainees from 80 countries participated in 160 courses, individual studies, or observation tours. In addition some 1,700 trainees participated in 61 local courses held in 20 countries. Most of the courses have been held in English, French, or Spanish, as well as in six other languages, including Turkish, Persian, and Rumanian. In addition, enriched by its own wide experience in the field, the department is advising other cooperation agencies on problems of methodology in training and education. It has specialized in short courses; its experiences have been analyzed in a comprehensive study.[4] The duration of its courses is usually from one to six months, most of them from three to four. Training breaks down into four parts, some parts offered simultaneously: learning special problems of the family farm; acquiring relevant theoretical knowledge; practical work in extension, including the student's accompanying of an officer designated as a tutor; assistance to the trainee in preparing an action plan on his return home.

Plans of action are discussed by the group and evaluated according to generally accepted criteria. Ideally, recommended changes are simple, feasible, inexpensive, and of direct benefit to the local farmer. It is stressed that one of the most essential criteria of the acceptability of a given change is maximal use of local resources. Local sources of information must be used as much as possible to avoid erroneous, unacceptable generalized recommendations made without specific knowledge of or relevance to local conditions. It is urged that local farmers and local leaders be employed as factors of change and innovation. Although changes should be introduced gradually and begin on a small scale, their application should be wide, aiming not at isolated, especially qualified, individuals but at wider units, such as villages or regions.

Particular emphasis is placed on techniques of training and education. A wide range of audiovisual aids is demonstrated, from the most elementary to the more sophisticated. Group discussion is also an important technique. Special importance is attached to course-long experimentation and demonstration whose culminating point is a field day. This practice is widely accepted by Israel's Ministry of Agriculture. Farmers from a large area are invited to observe and participate in an elaborate and well-prepared demonstration and exhibition in which a wide range of innovations are shown. This practice presents in a concentrated and accomplished manner what extension officers have taught during an entire season. As a part of their final exercise, foreign students plan and organize a complete field day. In their case it is composed of a number of agricultural experiments and demonstrations, such as the effect of different fertilizers, the introduction of new plant varieties, or the construction of poultry sheds from local materials. Each demonstration is illustrated or explained by written or spoken materials, with emphasis placed on the suitability of various innovations or experiments to hypothetical situations in the students' own countries.

The importance attached to educational programs stems from the conviction that the primary objective of training in Israel is to achieve the highest possible multiplier effect. The trainees must leave the country convinced that changes can be achieved, as proved by Israel's example, and that they possess the necessary techniques to implement them. They also should understand that a sense of mission and enthusiasm is a necessary condition for achieving meaningful changes in any community.

In recent years, in order to expand the number of trainees beyond existing facilities for conducting courses, Israel has encouraged the increases of local courses with Israeli participation. Teams of two or three—very seldom more—Israeli instructors conduct courses in receiving countries. Their chief advantages are their superior adaptability to local conditions, a much greater number of participants, and access to fuller cooperation in their organization and teaching with local governments. A good illustration is a course held in Gambia.[5] Following his visit to Israel, the director-general of the Gambian Ministry of Agriculture requested that a course for extension officers be held in his land. Thirty-six extension officers participated in a three-week course, in the middle of which a seminar was held for senior personnel of the ministry. This program, plus the fact that the members of the senior staff participated in the ordinary course as teachers and instructors, created a very favorable climate for improved contact among the various echelons of the ministry.

Local courses are being held whenever practicable to increase the technical and managerial capacity in projects assisted by Israeli consultants. In conjunction with extension services or other suitable branches of local administration, courses were held in Zambia, the Ivory Coast, Chile, and Peru. The experts employed on the project participated in the course as instructors with officials of local administration and Israelis sent especially for the course. This is an example of an integrated project, which combines training both in Israel and in the recipient country.

Local courses are also offered by other agencies, including the Afro-Asian Institute and the Centre for Labour and Cooperation Studies. In 1971 the Mount Carmel International Training Centre for Community Services introduced the complementary program of "in-country training" and thus arrived at a synthesis of Israel-based courses and local courses. The results up to now have been very favorable. Teachers and advisors from developing countries have also been invited in a number of cases, and there is an intention to expand this practice. Apart from their personal experience of training in Israel, they bring with them a knowledge of local conditions. In numerous cases the teachers invited have been former trainees of the same institutions, including the Department of Foreign Training of the Ministry of Agriculture and the Afro-Asian Institute for Cooperation and Labour Studies. Their success was striking precisely because they could refer directly to application of their own studies in Israel to the realities of their own countries.

The present range of courses is very wide. In addition to those already mentioned, they include social medicine in rural areas and industrial management, both for trainees from Latin America. In the past a number of successful courses in education were held for school inspectors in Tanzania, Kenya, and Uganda, or for functionaries in local government.

Preoccupation with follow-up of training in Israel was evident as early as 1965 in the formation of Shalom clubs. It was suggested that in each country alumni of any training institution in Israel should form a club for exchange of information and follow-up activities. A publication, *Shalom*, appears in English, French, and Spanish. The activities of Shalom clubs differ in intensity and character from country to country. An interesting innovation in Colombia, Chile, and Bolivia, for example, were symposia on problems of Latin American and national development organized by Shalom clubs in 1971 and 1972. In Bolivia the local Shalom club began publication in 1972 of its own periodical, *Tiempos Nuevos*. In other countries Shalom clubs are active in the promotion of cultural and scientific exchange with Israel. Everywhere particular attention is being paid to avoiding any political element in these clubs. Main stress is always placed on strengthening the ties with the training institute in Israel on professional issues.

The feeling still exists that too few follow-up activities with former trainees are being conducted. Among the possibilities considered for the future are increased participation in courses in Israel by candidates directly involved in development projects with Israel's cooperation. This, it is believed, would ensure a greater impact of cooperation assistance and would result in built-in follow-up. Training institutions could establish closer ties with former trainees by supplying information on innovations in their field of training. Itinerant refresher courses combined with evaluation and selection of candidates for future courses and symposia, similar to those held in Latin America in 1972, also seem to be practicable. Because of the relatively substantial efforts in terms of money and manpower that generally go into technical assistance programs, it would appear justified on the part of both donor and recipient nations to ensure necessary resources for adequate follow-up and periodic updating of the respective field of action or study.

Israeli projects, essentially technical assistance programs and not capital assistance, were from their inception based on bilateral agreements. At the same time there has always been a disposition, wherever practical and desired by the receiving nation, to coordinate them with other national or international development agencies. Israeli policies in this area preceded the recommendations for the Second Development Decade (1971-80) to bring about a major coordination of the activities of various donors. Such coordination, prima facie, can assure the intended cohesion and swift implementation of each project, as in any bilateral effort, and overall, objectively sound, general, problem-oriented direction of the whole complex —direction ordinarily expected from a multilateral enterprise. Actual projects of this type abroad are tripartite medical research projects in Nairobi, with the participation of Kenya, the Netherlands, and Israel, and the Centre of Vocational Training Aids in Bangkok, with the participation of Thailand, Israel, the International Labour Organization, and the U.N. Development Program (UNDP). In Israel a number of courses are conducted as a joint venture by Israel and development agencies, including UNDP, the Common Market, FAO, UNESCO, the World Meteorological Organization, the Swedish International Development Agency, and the Dutch Agency for International Cooperation.

Many characteristics of Israeli technical assistance have their origin in Israel's own position as a developing nation. At the 1970 Truman Conference, which was devoted to analysis of the needs of technical assistance, a recommendation was made that the specifics of assistance between developing countries themselves be studied.[6] Until 1973, at least, it would appear that this challenge has been met neither in Israel nor elsewhere. In the 1972 U.N. General Assembly this subject was again raised. A group of countries, including Argentina, Bolivia, Colombia, Costa Rica, Upper Volta, and Uruguay, in the course of discussion of the report of the Governing Council of UNDP, presented a resolution that "invited the Governing Council of UNDP to convene ... a working group in order to examine and make recommendations on the best way for developing countries to share their capacities and experience with one another, with a view to increasing and improving development assistance."[7]

NOTES

1. E. W. Martin, *1970 Review, Development Assistance, Efforts and Policies of the Members of the Development Assistance Committee* (Paris: OECD, December 1970), p. 17.

2. I have discussed these criteria at the Truman Conference. See *Proceedings of the*

Truman International Conference on Technical Assistance and Development (Jerusalem: The Harry S. Truman Research Institute, Hebrew University, 1970), pp. 50-63.

3. Dr. N. Chazan, *Function of Preliminary Training in Process of Israel's Assistance* (Jerusalem: Hebrew University, July 1972), provisional draft in Hebrew.

4. D. Makarov and G. Fradkin, *A Short Course to Development* (Ramat Gan; Massada, 1973).

5. Ibid., p. 161.

6. See *Proceedings of the Truman Conference*, op. cit., foreword by Ernst D. Bergman.

7. Document A/C.2/L.1263/Rev. 1, November 30, 1972

Israel's first official projects of technical cooperation with Burma and Ghana were initiated in 1955 and 1956. They were executed pursuant to a decision of the Ministry for Foreign Affairs and financed by its regular budget. Small in scale, they could be included in the ministry's normal schedule of work without obligating it to request extraordinary funds.

A small allocation for technical assistance in the normal budget of the Ministry for Foreign Affairs appeared for the first time as early as 1954-55. Given the facts that the Israeli fiscal year begins on April 1 and the preparation of the national budget extends over a period of approximately six months, it must be assumed that the decision to request an allocation for technical assistance was already made in the middle of 1953.

The scarcity of data pertaining to the budgeting and financing of Israeli technical assistance, especially during its early years, makes it very difficult to reach meaningful conclusions regarding the development and scope of technical assistance projects. (See Appendix A.)

After an initial fragmentary budget of $94,700 for fiscal 1958-59, allocations mounted steadily, reaching $5,285,000 in 1963. Since then the yearly budget for technical assistance has grown only slowly in terms of dollars, although statistics show an approximate doubling in Israeli pound expenditures, which was caused by the nation's series of devaluations.

The 1972-73 budget of 25 million Israeli pounds increased to 27 million because of a general cost-of-living adjustment equivalent to about $6.5 million. This sum represents roughly 50-60 percent of the total expenditure on international assistance. Because of different methods of obtaining and processing of relevant statistics, it is very hard to ascertain other components and arrive at an exact figure for the total sum. It can be assumed that the total official development cooperation of Israel amounts yearly to some $10 million, thus comparing favorably, in proportion, with several countries in the West.

The total number of Israeli technical experts in the last few years has reached about 500 annually, approximately 165 per million population. This figure compares with 1971 figures of approximately 250 experts per million population in countries of the Common Market and 100 in the United States.[1]

Among these 500 experts have been approximately 250 long-term (one-year) experts, 150 short-term experts serving on the basis of bilateral agreements, and about 100 in developing countries serving in the U.N. Development Program and other specialized agencies. The yearly average of students and trainees in Israel during the last few years has been some 1,300, including about 150 in periods of study of a year or more and 200 in study tours of a few weeks' duration. The majority took courses of three to six months' duration. In the last few years there has been an increase of participants in local, "on-the-spot" courses in receiving countries. In 1972, for example, local courses were held with more than 1,000 trainees participating. (See Appendix B).

Despite the number and diversity of Israel's projects, agriculture and the problems of rural society remain its central concerns. In these fields there is a convergence of need and expertise—need in the developing countries, specific experience and expertise in Israel. More than half of Israel's technical cooperation projects at home and abroad are related to agriculture and rural society. Statistically agriculture is also a main component of sectors classified as cooperation, community development, and youth activities.

The primary characteristics of the main sectors of Israeli technical assistance have already been described and analyzed. Some, like medicine, however, while they have been referred to tangentially in a specific context, have actually involved highly important, successful, and interesting assistance projects, including the training of nurses.[2] Vocational training, too, has been considered here only in terms of youth programs, although elaborate projects in this field were conducted at home in a great vocational center in Netanya. At the request of the Organization of American States courses have been held in public housing and industrial productivity. In addition, to meet changing needs efforts are being made to train adequate teaching personnel and prepare curricula in subjects such as financing urban development and involving the private sector in national development.

Apart from sectors of a repetitive nature or those that enabled the Israel cooperation administration to gear itself to projects of a lasting nature, there have been numerous instances of successful projects of a unique character, especially in a number of African countries in which Israeli advisors arrived soon after the countries' independence. Informal relations, geographic proximity, a relatively simple decision-making process, and Israel's own experience in improvisation resulted in a series of "firsts" in these nations in fields apart from agriculture, community development, health, and youth programs. In Guinea, Israel assisted in designing and printing the nation's first stamps. In Chad and Togo, Israelis assisted in mounting the first printing press and editing the first daily newspaper there. Among other successful ventures introduced in several African countries have been national lotteries following the accepted pattern of Israel's, using the proceeds to finance hospitals and community centers. Other "firsts" have included rather less popular innovations, such as the purchase tax in Tanzania and Uganda.

The geographic distribution of assistance projects both at home and abroad demonstrates the preponderance of Africa in Israeli technical assistance programs. In the first decade of Israel's assistance programs (1958-67), two-thirds of its experts —about 1,700 of a total of over 2,500—served in Africa. In 1969 the proportion was still more than half, or some 250 out of a total of 465.[3] The proportion of trainees was about half, or some 5,300 out of 10,500, during 1967-68 and about one-third, or 475 out of 1,300, in 1969.[4]

The high proportion of cooperation projects in African countries has several causes. With the exception of Burma, most projects began in Africa. Geographically, of course, Africa is the area nearest to Israel, at least for all practical purposes so long as the Arab world maintains a state of war with Israel. The overriding reasons for Africa's preeminence in this area, however, are its immense needs and the volume of its aid requests to Israel, as well as Israel's proven will to meet these requests, a disposition nurtured primarily by immediate, humanitarian considerations.

During 1972 Israel's state of warfare with the Arabs affected its relations with several African countries. Its relations with Uganda ended abruptly and dramatically following President Idi Amin's visit to Libya. Chad, Niger, Mali, and Republic of the Congo (Brazzaville) also severed their ties with Israel in that year. Any evaluation of this development or prognosis is outside the scope of this work. Suffice it to say that cessation of diplomatic relations led to cessation of projects of technical cooperation.

Israeli technical aid to Asia embraces projects in Nepal, Thailand, Laos, Cambodia, Singapore, the Philippines, and Korea. A substantial number of countries, including Ceylon (Sri Lanka), do not maintain diplomatic relations with Israel and thus do not participate in its technical cooperation projects. In some nations, such as India, limited projects of coopeation are maintained. Some Israeli experts have served in India under U.N. auspices and Indian trainees frequently participate in courses in Israel (usually under the sponsorship of nongovernmental organizations). In countries in which Israel maintains technical assistance programs, with the exception of the Philippines and its Christian background, the interest in technical cooperation with Israel is devoid of any even partially shared cultural heritage. Technical assistance, therefore, is necessarily based on a receiving nation's recognition of Israel's practical achievement and expertise in economic and technological fields and its interest in adapting Israeli techniques to its own needs. The lessons of Israeli in rapid economic growth and steady social development are the prime interest of these countries.

Participating nations in the Middle East and the eastern Mediterranean area include Cyprus, Greece, Turkey, and Iran, all of which, in many ways, have a geographical and cultural affinity with Israel that would justify a wide spectrum of cooperation projects. Here again political considerations, chiefly apprehension regarding possible negative Arab reactions, have sometimes precluded open cooperation projects between these countries and Israel. Statistics in this area quite naturally reflect this apprehension and ambivalence.

Israeli projects in Latin America were initiated later than elsewhere, but they have been increasing in size and number. Cultural, historic, and religious factors dating back far beyond the formation of the state of Israel have encouraged a sustained interest in and sympathy for Israel that have led to very gratifying projects of cooperation, especially in the fields of agriculture and comprehensive regional planning. A relatively high level of general development in various sectors enabled Latin American nations to absorb and adapt Israeli experience and techniques with notable success and rapidity. From the very beginning of the projects, suggested Israeli concepts were warmly received by national authorities, who, in most cases, arranged for requisite institutional support. On the regional level very beneficial relations were established with the OAS and the Inter-American Development Bank. Formal agreements and detailed work plans were established to define technical assistance programs of genuine significance to interested governments. Sustained institutional support both by governments and by Inter-American organizations is a main reason for the success of projects in Latin America.

The operational unit in the Ministry for Foreign Affairs responsible for the project cooperation activities of Israel is the Division for International Cooperation (DIC). It performs a dual function that in other countries—in several analogous cases—is conducted by two separate units, a policy-forming section and a more independent executive agency. The first function of the DIC is to advise the ministry as to the most effective and judicious ways of carrying out cooperation projects. Toward this end it maintains close contact with Israeli diplomatic missions abroad and with appropriate geographical departments in the Israeli Ministry for Foreign Affairs. This close communication in thc field enables the DIC constantly to be aware of the needs and expectations of receiving governments and the opinions of the respective Israeli institutions. The acute problem of establishing priorities of allocation among countries and continents is therefore not restricted to, let us say, a single decision or a yearly examination of forthcoming budget allocations. The decision-making process is taking place during the daily, continuous implementation of fieldwork. Since almost without exception the fieldwork of Israeli experts is supervised either by the ambassador or a member of his staff, and not by a special cooperation project chief, communication between field men and headquarters is both direct and swift.

The second function performed by the DIC is that of an administrative organ of the Ministry for Foreign Affairs in cooperation projects. In the performance of this role it is responsible for the preparation of the budget and disbursement of allocations; the selection and formulation of projects according to continent, country, and sector of activity; the selection of professional executive agencies; the elaboration of rules and procedures for servicing experts abroad; the admission of trainees and students at home; and the performance of the vast number of essential staff functions falling under the general term "evaluation and follow-up."

The DIC, or *Mashav*, an acronym for the Hebrew *Makhlaka Leshituf Beinlumi*, in 1972 numbered about 35 staff members, of whom 15 were on the diplomatic staff and the rest were administrative or clerical employees. Officers are in charge of geographical divisions or of such special functions as training, manpower, publications, and reporting. Until 1968 *Mashav* retained special liaison officers in charge of such sectoral activities as agriculture and medicine, but later this function was discontinued. Professional work, such as the direction and preparation of agricultural or other specific activities, is performed by professional centers whose directors and members serve as direct advisors to the *Mashav* director and its other members in the areas of their special competence.

The International Agricultural Cooperation Centre, in Rehovot, is the largest professional agency. It employed some 27 people in 1972, most of them agricultural planners, agronomists, and agricultural economists. Apart from lending professional staff support to agricultural projects abroad, including reference libraries and training centers for future experts, the Centre often provides actual field services in projects, principally in physical and economic planning when experts in a project are of differing disciplines. It also helps to coordinate research activities of the projects.

The Foreign Training Department of the Extension Service of the Ministry of Agriculture is another large specialized agency in the cooperation system of Israel. In 1972 it had 21 employees carrying out training programs in Israel and abroad. (See Chapter 9.) The International Youth Cooperation Center, until 1972 part of the Ministry of Defense, became an independent unit guided professionally by a board of specialists. This center and the Mount Carmel International Training Centre for Community Services, which specializes in training programs for women from developing countries, are constitutionally dependencies of the Israel Association for International Cooperation. This association was formed in 1962 by the Ministry for Foreign Affairs as a public body with the participation of nongovernmental representatives, hopefully to lend its activities broad public support and to promote general interest in its activities. Future plans call for the transfer of still other functions of cooperation to this association.

Other specialized organizations involved in cooperation projects are the Afro-Asian Institute and the Centre for Labour Studies and Cooperation. In other fields, when the scope of activities is not great enough to warrant the establishment of a special unit, professional advice and supervision are provided either by part-time consultants or through *ad hoc* arrangements. Such arrangements obtain in the cases of advisors on health and medicine and science and technology, in addition to various cooperation projects executed on a basis of subcontracting.

The present *Mashav* system, with its compact staff, full-time or part-time specialized professional units, and *ad hoc* subcontracting agencies has several advantages. Above all it is flexible, enabling the Israeli system to adjust to changing needs with relative freedom from the burden of past commitments. Its principal disadvantage, however, lies in its constant need to mobilize new agencies and hire people for new projects. This of course is an especially difficult challenge in a state of overemployment. It is possible that formation of a larger nucleus of officers trained in professions in fields that will require Israeli cooperation for many years to come and complementing this professional nucleus with *ad hoc* personnel could provide the optimal solution to present difficulties.

In the operations of *Mashav* as a staff unit, various functions are constantly being revised. In 1972, for example, an updating and evaluation unit was established, with the objective of assuring greater uniformity and meaning to reporting procedures. This is especially important because joint yearly reviews with receiving countries and the formulation of long-term planning procedures are becoming an urgent need.

NOTES

1. See E. W. Martin, *1972 Review, Development Cooperation, Efforts and Policies of the Members of the Development Assistance Committee* (Paris: OECD, December 1972), pp. 234-35.

2. See Judith Steiner, *Evaluation of Training Programs for African Nurses* (Jerusalem: Hebrew University Hadassah Medical School, 1970).

3. *Israel Programme of International Cooperation* (Jerusalem: Division of International Cooperation, 1970), p. 56.

4. Ibid, p. 58.

With reference to Israeli activities in developing countries, among friends and foes, there exists a certain ambiguity in the use of the term "assistance." This term, especially when used by one critically inclined, indicates *all* activities related in any way to Israel or Israelis, even when it does not encompass accepted norms of technical assistance or cooperation.

It is useful, therefore, to define the term "assistance" as it has been used in this text, at least broadly. As conceived here it is meant to indicate official projects of cooperation; works and projects conducted by Israeli firms and/or individuals; and activities carried out with the aid or intervention of Israelis or former Israelis, usually residing abroad, without elements of Israeli know-how, financing, or implementation.

Official cooperation projects are those, of course, formally agreed upon by participating governments. Indiscriminately they include a great element on the part of Israel. Practically all of these projects are in the area of technical assistance, in sectors designated by a receiving government in terms of its national developmental priorities. It is these projects that have constituted the central subject matter of this book thus far.

Works or projects carried out abroad by Israeli firms or individuals have to be approved by the controller of foreign exchange in the Ministry of Finance. Most of the projects are conducted by a small number of large, long-established Israeli consulting or contracting companies with subsidiary operations abroad, chiefly in developing countries. In recent years a number of smaller Israeli firms or individuals have entered this field in developing countries, some of them successfully. Prominent among their activities have been planning and consultancy in architecture, construction, agriculture, regional planning, engineering, and irrigation.

Given the high priority of such projects in the economy of developing countries and the fact that in most cases contracting firms are at least partially controlled by the Israeli government or a recognized public organization like *Histadrut*, they have often been loosely described as "assistance." While there is certainly justification for this definition, considered broadly, it should be remembered that these firms do operate on a business basis and quite naturally compete with other firms internationally. The origin and scope of these economic activities are the subject matter of this chapter.

In several countries projects have been carried out through the intervention and promotion of individual Israelis, some of whom do not even reside in Israel any more. They have acted on behalf of non-Israeli firms that do not require approval of the Israeli controller of foreign exchange. In several instances such Israeli or ex-Israeli promoters have contracted with Israeli experts and other individuals, altogether privately, to fill some posts. A typical case might be that of an Israeli or ex-Israeli promoter initiating, say, construction of a hotel by a non-Israeli firm and later engaging Israelis to fill vacancies in the project's management. Such ventures have in some cases proved to be very successful; in others they have not. This kind of project, executed by Israeli nationals without official assistance or approval or even knowledge by the controller of foreign exchange, is not within the scope of the present chapter. The distinction between activities of this category and the former is to a degree artificial and not always justified. Because official guidance in such projects is almost nonexistent, however, a line of demarcation has been suggested, only so that such projects directed by Israelis residing abroad would not be included under the broader, umbrella term "Israeli assistance" as it has been used generically in this book.

It should be recalled that developmental projects were initiated by Israeli corporations much earlier than they were initiated under official government aegis —indeed, in some instances, before the state of Israel was established. The Jewish Palestinian population for a long time enjoyed a considerable concentration of skilled manpower in technology, sciences, and various disciplines that was not always utilized to its full capacity. Indeed, during World War II in many key fields Palestinian Jewish skills were a mainstay of the Allied war effort throughout the Middle East. During the war the composition of the Palestinian Jewish labor force was transformed, industry replacing agriculture as the leading occupation.[1] Jewish engineers participated in a number of major projects of the Allied war effort throughout the Middle East, principally in road building and other forms of public construction.

Following the establishment of the state of Israel in 1948, for a number of years there was a need for all available technical personnel to restore or reconstruct facilities devastated by war and to construct new projects required mainly by mass immigration. Housing projects, transforming temporary "transit camps" into more permanent dwellings, were constructed at feverish speed. Public buildings, schools, health clinics, and shopping centers were designed and erected in urban and rural areas. Massive infrastructure projects, especially in the development of water resources, a new electricity grid, and an expanded network of roads not only helped to meet immense new demands on the Israeli economy but also occasioned changes in the character and responsibilities of its labor force.

Mass immigration to Israel reached its peak in the early 1950s. In the middle of that decade some professional personnel, notably in hydraulic engineering, gradually approached completion of major development projects. For example, a milestone in the developmental history of Israel was the successful completion of the National Water Carrier. A major engineering enterprise, considered even on an international scale, this project provided for the elevation of waters of the River Jordan from the Sea of Galilee for use in southern Israel to a height of 400 meters (440 yards)—200 kilometers (124 miles) away. The quantity of water thus carried per year—some 350 million cubic meters (458 million cubic yards) represents approximately one-quarter of the total water available in Israel for all uses.

The completion of these development projects presented executing agencies with the alternatives of transferring their skilled engineering staffs to different occupations or seeking outlets for further use of their expertise. At the same time, other developing nations achieved independence and were naturally interested in initiating their own developmental projects. They disposed of reserves inherited from colonial powers and manifested a keen interest in Israel in terms of its own developmental experience and challenges and those of its official projects of technical assistance that might be applied in their interest on perhaps a smaller scale.

The three firms with the most ambitious projects in the developing countries during the late 1950s through the 1960s were Solel Boneh (Paver and Builder) in construction, WRD (Water Resources Development), and TAHAL (Water Planning and Consultants). ZIM (Israel Merchant Navigation) was instrumental in the creation of navigational companies in Ghana and Burma. Three of these companies —excluding TAHAL—formed joint companies in some countries that at one stage represented an original, dynamic form of cooperation.

Solel Boneh, one of the main economic enterprises of *Histadrut*, originated in the 1920s and became the largest general contractor in Palestine—later in Israel— in civil engineering, housing, and road building. During World War II it performed a large number of works for the Allies in several countries of the Middle East and earned a high reputation for great reliability and fine workmanship. The experience it gained in works and projects abroad was further utilized when in 1945 it established a joint company with a Cypriote firm (CYBARCO) that continues to operate successfully. It has carried out a number of important developmental projects, including airfields, dams, harbors, and public buildings.

In 1958 Solel Boneh was reorganized. Among other changes in its structure, a special subsidiary for foreign operations was established—Solel Boneh Overseas and Harbors Ltd. Within 10 years it was operating in 14 foreign countries in the Middle East, Asia, Africa, and Latin America. In the same decade the monetary value of its completed works increased annually from $6.4 million to $32 million.

The director of Solel Boneh Overseas, Yaacov Shur, has on several occasions discussed the achievements, challenges, and problems of his company. Of particular interest have been his statements regarding the motivation of his company and its contribution to the economy of Israel and the development of other countries. His views reflect to a considerable degree the attitudes of other large Israeli firms active in developing countries.

In celebrating the twenty-fifth anniversary of Solel Boneh's foreign operations in 1969, Mr. Shur observed: "This activity didn't start accidentally; neither did it grow by chance. It was a synthesis of several positive characteristics that guided the activities toward established goals. These characteristics are vision and practical approach, an economic venture with a humanitarian and moral impetus, aiming at projects that will be profitable and at the same time will bring welfare and eliminate exploitation. . . . This combination is based upon the social tradition of Solel Boneh and on its comprehensive philosophy, deeply rooted in the essential values of the Israeli labor movement."[2]

Solel Boneh's activities abroad during its formative years, Mr. Shur observed, were distinguished by their "fostering human relations and labor relations in different places, designing a system of contacts that sees the local personnel as a partner in a challenge. . . . The disposition to implant roots on the spot, to live with local people even in far-away corners, to learn their language, and to understand the local man directly—all these . . . created an attitude of sympathy and good-will. In labor relations emphasis was placed upon good treatment, speedy improvement of social conditions, welfare, and training and promotion of employees."

The extent to which Solel Boneh's objectives and modalities were put into practice is difficult to assess. The very fact that they could have been presented so frankly in a public address, however, supports the belief that Solel Boneh considered itself as an organization with a mission, not simply as a profit-making enterprise. It is difficult to conceive of contracting firms in other nations making such idealistic statements publicly in their own countries. Indeed, Solel Boneh's prospectus unequivocally states its mission as serving as an instrument of progress abroad: "On all projects Solel Boneh's method of operation is based on the broad principle of international cooperation. Although it brings its own experts to the job, it makes the fullest possible use of local manpower in implementation, and it employs locally available materials to the greatest possible extent."[3]

In assessing the economic advantages to Israel of Solel Boneh's operations, its managing director has expressed much less satisfaction.[4] He estimated that out of the total average yearly operation in the 1960s—over $30 million gross—not more than 10 percent represented earnings in foreign exchange. This figure included the export of Israeli goods and equipment generated by the project in planning and services, including financing, insurance, profit, and personal savings. He considered this sum to be very low, especially in view of the unsatisfactory amount of Israeli goods and services used in the project.

This issue of "added value," or foreign exchange earnings in projects abroad, was and is one of critical importance for interested companies, one directly related to problems of financing and insurance. Israeli regulations as a rule permit insurance of only double the amount of Israeli export of goods and services to projects abroad. Even if these components reach twice the percentage cited, or 20 percent, the total amount insured would be only 40 percent, or less than half the total cost of the project. In such cases, even if the company were able to finance a project out of its own resources or from available credits, its limited eligibility for insurance would present serious difficulties.

In retrospect, it would appear that Solel Boneh has succeeded in striking a balance between its commercial interests and the more altruistic objectives of international cooperation. It has not only served as a development agency on a *de facto* basis in the exercise of its business activities but in several cases has held quite sophisticated on-the-job training projects for several levels of employees. Although its earnings in foreign exchange have not met its expectations, often because of limited opportunities available to Israeli exporters, its projects have utilized valuable Israeli goods and services, mainly planning.

In recent years Solel Boneh has preferred to operate independently rather than through associated companies. Among the reasons for this is that in several countries in which revolutions have occurred, the local partner of Solel Boneh became identified with the deposed regime—with occasional and obvious adverse effects on Solel Boneh itself. In some countries the firm's activities were curtailed either because of the lack of additional developmental budgets or because of political changes. At the same time the firm, secure in its sense of mission, simply started operations in new countries. In some countries, notably those with advanced services and techniques of their own—like Argentina and Venezuela—successful continuation of Solel Boneh projects proved not only the high quality of its services but also the effective presence of elements of technical cooperative assistance.

Water Resources Development, Ltd. (WRD) was established in 1958 as a subsidiary of *Mekoroth* (Sources), the national company that carried out extensive projects in the development of water resources, including the famed National Water Carrier cited earlier. WRD operated either independently or in partnership with a local firm in nine countries in Africa, the Middle East, and Latin America. In several countries, including Nigeria, in which its project of urban water supply was widespread, the firm gained a fine reputation for precision and efficiency. The benefits of local goodwill accrued not only to it as a viable concern but also to the state of Israel, whose very name became associated with water supply for direct human consumption and for irrigation.

In the late 1960s WRD became involved in road building and housing, areas not within the expertise and experience of its mother company. The principal reason for this shift was WRD's belief that it would more effectively utilize its human and material resources. As a consequence of this venture, however, the company faced several administrative and managerial problems and suffered from limitations in financial resources that obliged it to obtain credit on unfavorable terms. In two big development projects—road building in Peru and dam construction in Iran—it accepted firm engagements without making adequate preliminary studies, with the result that it incurred heavy operational losses. In Israel itself the company's unfortunate financial situation created widespread reaction in 1972. The Knesset requested an inquiry into its operations by the state comptroller, who reported insufficient preliminary studies and administrative deficiencies as the basic reasons for the company's financial crisis. As a result the Israeli government discontinued the independent existence of the company and transferred its assets—and accrued goodwill—to Solel Boneh.

From 1959 to 1971 WRD was involved in operations accounting for about $160 million, with losses estimated at approximately $20 million. Here again the human element was placed before the economic. Despite very tangible losses for the Israeli economy resulting from WRD's projects, the firm's operations abroad proved successful, of value to local populations because of their high quality in the vital areas of direct human water consumption and irrigation.

TAHAL (Water Planning for Israel) was founded in 1952 by merging the Technical Department of *Mekoroth* with the Irrigation and Drainage Department of the Ministry of Agriculture. TAHAL's function was to plan and organize the general water resources of Israel, more specifically to plan in detail for the needs of national, regional, and local water networks. When the National Water Carrier neared completion in the late 1950s, TAHAL started to search for foreign markets. Its search broadly paralleled the development of Israel's diplomatic relations. The first projects undertaken by TAHAL were in Ghana and Burma, followed by contracts in western and eastern Nigeria and other countries in Africa, Asia, and the Middle East. In the mid-1960s the firm began operations in Asia and Latin America. During its early years TAHAL's projects were concerned mainly with urban water supply, shifting later to irrigation and agricultural development, including comprehensive planning and training.

TAHAL's largest project was undertaken in Ghazvin, Iran (see Chapter 4). As early as 1961 it had received an FAO contract to conduct a hydrological survey and develop a training service for local personnel. When the area was affected by an earthquake of extraordinary magnitude in 1962, TAHAL was commissioned by FAO to plan and supervise the reconstruction of the water supply system and by the Plan Organization of the Iranian government to prepare a comprehensive plan for the agricultural development of the Ghazvin area. At one stage work on the Iranian project represented up to 40 percent of TAHAL's activities abroad.

Between 1960 and 1970 TAHAL's works abroad approximated the sum of $25 million. Because the company is concerned only with planning, consultation, and functions of supervision, and not with carrying out big construction work, done by contractors, its turnover is relatively light, but of a high added value (earned foreign exchange transferred to Israel)—up to 50 percent. This is one of the major differences between TAHAL and contractors like Solel Boneh, whose operations are considerably larger, including a much higher element of local cost but offering lower added value.

TAHAL's programs continue to be vital in various parts of the world. Given the growing use of water for direct human consumption, industry, and agriculture, there is a concomitantly growing preoccupation with implementing the most efficient master plans and ensuring optimal water utilization throughout the world. In temperate climates supplementary irrigation is being gradually introduced. Experimental, innovative methods of water preservation and continuing efforts to advance research in water desalinization have become a preoccupation of many countries that until recently scarcely assumed that they might suffer from a water shortage. The primary targets for future water utilization, however, are the vast tracts of desert that occupy almost one-third of the land area of the globe and have naturally become a new frontier for mankind. A precondition of conquering this frontier, however, is a major breakthrough in introducing unconventional methods of providing additional water supply. These problems and challenges are the subjects of constant research and experimentation in academic and operational establishments in Israel, establishments with which TAHAL is intimately connected in its work both at home and abroad.

In 1972 TAHAL was engaged in 27 projects in 14 developing countries in Africa, Asia, Europe, and Latin America. A U.N. Development Program project of comparative studies of irrigation in five Latin American countries, inspired by TAHAL, was under active consideration and study in the IDB, the executive agent of the UNDP. The book *The Role of Water in Development Planning*, written by TAHAL's president,[5] provides an outline of a comprehensive planning approach and its application to various uses of water for urban and rural consumption. TAHAL has also been commissioned to prepare national, subnational, and regional water inventories that have served as bases for master water plans in several countries.

In recent years a number of smaller firms have undertaken projects in agricultural planning and consultation in various subjects on a business basis. *Agridev* (Agricultural Development) has for years maintained a management contract with Motoragri, a company controlled by the Ministry of Agriculture of the Ivory Coast for the maintenance and operation of heavy agricultural machinery. Koor Projects, a subsidiary of *Histadrut's* industrial concern, Koor (Furnace), is a partner in agricultural projects—cotton production in Ethiopia and the growing of cattle feed in Zambia—and plans additional activities in industry and service in developing countries. In Venezuela projects of comprehensive planning have been undertaken by an Israeli firm on a commercial basis. In building, construction, and architecture other Israeli firms have begun operations abroad, among them the Rassco Construction Company, which has enjoyed a prestigious performance record in Israel dating back to the 1930s, and the Federman Company, active for years in hotel, housing, and industry.

A number of joint ventures have also been undertaken in technological and industrial fields. The motivation for their undertaking has often been the prospect of establishing an export channel for Israeli-made components for local coproduction. This is what induced an Israeli pharmaceutical firm to conduct a joint venture with a partner in an African country. In another case an exporter of ready-made raincoats faced the possibility of restrictions and even prohibition on the importation of finished goods to a certain country, established a factory there, and imported from Israel only the textile, or semifinished, goods. The factory, besides saving foreign exchange for the African country, generated almost one hundred jobs.

Most plans for industrial projects involving Israel exist or have existed in Africa. In spite of a continuing interest in these plans, however, only a few of them reach the implementation stage. The main obstacles to their realization have been lack of sufficient technical and managerial personnel in Israel to serve in an advisory capacity and a similar deficiency on the part of the receiving nation. Establishing a more efficient technical and managerial staff, essential in agriculture, is even more difficult to achieve in industrial and technological ventures because of their need for greater precision, sophistication, and continuity in production and maintenance.

Despite numerous attempts to export services and know-how, only a few Israeli firms, notably those mentioned, have succeeded in doing so on a large scale. Some successful ventures in this direction were made in the 1970s in Latin America in the fields of regional planning, mainly in Venezuela and Brazil. The Israeli government has attempted several times to assist smaller planning and consulting firms in their efforts to develop projects abroad. One such attempt, made in 1970, was the formation of the new Institute for Planning and Development by the Israeli government in conjunction with the Association of Engineers and Architects. The objectives of the Association are to build up an information center, to represent its members in related international organizations offering contracts, and to assist in the promotion of their exporting capacity in fields of planning that are of special interest to developing countries.

While there is a continuing and growing interest on the part of several firms in increasing their activity in developing countries, there is less interest in joint ventures in activities of major scale comparable with those of the early 1960s. In that period the joint company model was a very important and successful instrument of cooperation. It was used in building, construction, development of water resources, and navigation. The history of ZIM's (Israel National Navigation Company) cooperation with Ghana in creating the Black Star Line serves as an illustration of different modalities of the joint company. The initial stage of this venture was that of the genuine joint company, with ZIM entering into a direct partnership with the local government. As a rule Israelis have insisted on holding only a minority of shares, and they did so in Ghana. At a later stage the partnership became what was called a management contract. When the local partner decided that it was ready and willing to assume formal management of the project, ZIM was requested to serve in an advisory capacity. ZIM now serves as agent for Black Star in those countries in which the company does not need an independent representation, and this is the only formal relation between the companies. All other relations remain informal, based on personal relations built up during many years of fruitful association. A similar pattern of gradual phasing out from joint ventures to completely independent companies was followed in many other cases. On the whole it can be considered as a fruitful and original instrument of mutual relations in the history of Israel's cooperation abroad.

NOTES

1. Martin W. Wilmington, *The Middle East Supply Centre* (London: University of London Press, 1971), p. 107.

2. Address of Mr. J. Shur, managing director, September 1969, in Hebrew (unpublished).

3. Ibid.

4. Ibid.

5. A. Wiener, *The Role of Water in Development Planning* (New York: McGraw-Hill, 1972).

The central factors of Israel's own growth and development and their application to development problems abroad have been discussed, it is hoped, with both adequate detail and analysis to permit the reader a sounder grasp of their purposes, their successes, their failures, and their hopes for needed reform.

No book on this subject would be even nearly complete, however, without a discussion of the roots, the genesis, of modern Israel, of Judaism itself—for the one presupposes the other—most particularly with reference to the question of development cooperation. Although Israel has emerged as a revolutionary antithesis vis-à-vis the millennial existence of the Jewish nation in the Diaspora, it has deep roots in tradition and ideology of the Jewish nation as such and in Judaism. There is hardly a lasting feature of the modern state that has not some meaningful relation to an important tradition. This holds especially true for a political and moral set of values for Israel viewed as the state and society.

Perhaps the keystone in the arch of Israel's political ideology, in practice as well as in the abstract, is its tenacious quest for a code of conduct that is at once utterly practical and uncompromisingly ethical, a code of conduct that might be described as one of realizable idealism. The quest for this code of conduct began, in a sense, with the first word of Genesis and the story of man's dialogue with God, the struggle for freedom from Pharaoh's yoke in Exodus, the development of Jewish culture in the writings of the major and minor prophets, the evolution of Judaism in the period of the Second Temple, the emergence of exegetical commentary in the Talmudic era culminating in the creative ferment of rabbinical commentary, and the literature of our times. Always in the Jewish quest for workable ethics the desire to build a set of values that could be realized and complied with in everyday life, in what we call the "road of life," has been a prime mover.

To understand this quest for a workable ethic one need not flee into realms of mystical experience or asceticism. Indeed, as any student of the Bible recognizes immediately, a hallmark of Jewish history and Jewish religious evolution as described in the Scriptures is its intense practicality, the very humanness of its struggle, its continuing debates between temporal and sacred rulers, its winning honesty and candid doubt and wonder before the ultimate problems of the human experience. Nor does one need the services of a mediator to understand it. For Judaism places its hopes for man here on earth. In this respect the Bible is most explicit: "It is not in Heaven that thou shouldst say, who shall go up for us to heaven and bring it unto us that we may hear and do it. Neither is it beyond the sea that thou shouldst say, who shall go over the sea for us and bring it unto us that we may hear and do it. But the word is very nigh unto thee, in thy mouth and in thy heart that thou mayest do it."[1] Moses, the great Law-giver himself, in his farewell address to his people deems it proper to stress that the Law, the Torah, is not an arcane or esoteric creation and abstraction, but an open book, accessible to everyone.

An obvious concomitant of an ideology of realizable targets is the awareness that man can only do his best, that any form of fulfillment, in the very nature of man's personal and environmental limitations, must be limited and will fall short of desired goals. The Jewish way of life is pragmatic, accounting fully for human inadequacies and failures. At the same time it is demanding, impelled by unceasing efforts to progress, to excel, to attain higher goals within the "length of our days," goals set down by a continuing understanding and application of the Torah, the supreme ethical law, or goals acquired in the pursuit of learning. We pray, in the words of one Jewish book of worship, "that we may see and welcome all truth, whether shining from the annals of ancient revelations or reaching us through the seers of our own time," convinced that God "hidest not [His] light from any generation of [His] children that yearn for [Him] and seek [His] guidance."[2] Ethical laws, in short, were and will be set down for man not as he is but as he can become. Between life as it is and Utopia is a desirable, attainable norm: That is the Jewish ideal, the governing principle of Jewish conduct. We *do* not because we *cannot* expect the total realization of our ideals. But we can try. One great rabbi put it beautifully in the *Pirke Avot* (Sayings of the Fathers): "It is not thy duty to complete the work, but neither art thou free to desist from it."[3] Throughout Jewish religious and ethical teachings is this simultaneous stress on man's limits and duties, on the priority of actual deeds over theoretical knowledge, on the fulfillment over the proclamation of the Law—as vital as the latter might be—of *doing* over dogma.

The ideology of modern Israel, its candid mix of individual initiative and democratic socialism—a mix denigrated and despised by the doctrinaires both Left and Right—professes, therefore, not revolution but evolution—an attempt to improve, to transform the human condition through education, mutual help, and trust. It follows that because nothing is or can be perfect, it is futile to destroy an existing social structure uncritically or unselectively and arbitrarily establish a new one—which, as history demonstrates only too well, will doubtless have major faults of its own. Any change benefiting the society is a result of a prolonged process, not of a single act.

Another element central to the Jewish tradition, inherited by and embodied in the state of Israel, is the conception of society itself as a living, indivisible *organism*. This conception does not in any way deny the concrete existence of the individual *per se*; after all, he does exist, has an identity, rights, duties, aspirations. This conception of society insists, however, that the individual, in indisputable fact, can mature, can be realized only within society. It is true that in the period immediately preceding the destruction of the Herodian temple in Jerusalem by the Roman emperor Titus in 70 C. E. Jewish ascetic orders and self-abnegating hermits were known; but such groups and individuals were never popular among the Jews, never in the mainstream of their community. Even in the matter of prayer—and this condition still prevails and, indeed, is stressed—worship is ideally communal. This is not to say that individual prayer is either impermissible or to be discounted but that whenever possible, one should pray with one's community in a synagogue (from the Greek "place of meeting"). At least in Orthodox synagogues prayer cannot even begin unles a *minyan*, or group of ten males, is present, although this restriction has been lifted by Reform congregations and others.

Because man can attain self-realization and fulfillment only in society, he inevitably develops feelings of empathy, responsibility, and care for his neighbors, near and far, concepts of social justice, social equality, and compassion for all strata of society, especially for the poor and the underprivileged. Both the Bible (such as Deuteronomy 24:13) and the Talmud (rabbinical commentaries on the Bible) are very strict on the last count. Aid to the underprivileged must permit the recipient of aid or charity to keep face, must be given irrespective of his faith, or origin, and must be given with "tender words," which "may mean more to the poor," says one brilliant scholar, "than the gift itself."[4] (*T. Sukkah* 49b, Isidore Epstein, *Judaism*, Baltimore, Maryland: Penguin Books, p. 151).

Even in the earlier parts of the Bible, such as Genesis and Exodus, which are more narrative or historical and less homiletic than succeeding Scripture, a high degree of progression in social identification from family to tribe, to nation, and to the world at large is increasingly manifest. The prophetic vision of peace—a universal conversion of swords into ploughshares, culminating, of course, in Isaiah, has been achieved as early as the time of the first Temple.

In the post-temple era, from the sixth century onward, Jewish spiritual leaders were to be confronted by massive challenges to the Jewish identity and heritage by the Greek and Roman cultures. Essentially they were confronted with the problem of maintaining what they considered to be their special identity and at the same time coexisting amicably and maintaining mutual respect with their non-Jewish neighbors. They wished at once to remain uncompromisingly loyal to their beliefs and to get along with those whom they came to call "the pious of all nations." Rabbi Meir, for example, observed: "How do we know that a non-Jew dealing in the study of Torah, Law, Ethics, is equal to the High Priest? Because it is said in the Bible: "Ye shall therefore keep my statutes and my judgments, which if a man do, he shall live in them." The Bible says not "priests, Levites, and Israelites," but "Man." Hence one deduces that even a non-Jew, provided he deals in study of Law, is equal to the High Priest."[5] It is ironic that a concept of such vaulting universality should come from a spiritual leader of a people forbidden by tyrants even to study their faith—in private—on pain of death, as they were under Hadrian.

Today this Jewish concept of universality, its vision of one universal family of nations, obviously presupposes the need for universal peace and mutual responsibility and assistance to nations as a logical extension of a similar code of behavior within nations.

Modern Israel's attitude toward material goods is also rooted in Jewish heritage. We are not, to put a fine point on this once more, dealing here with asceticism, which is simply out of the mainstream of Jewish thought. What has been criticized both by the prophets and by their heirs has been waste and luxury for the few in the presence of poverty for the many. In Leviticus, for example, if we are urged not to "favor the poor," we are also told not to "show deference to the rich" but to "judge [our] neighbor fairly."[6] We are reminded in Deuteronomy that clothing and shelter are the *right* of the poor.[7] And a later commentary states that while a landowner has a natural and legitimate legal right in land ownership, all land is ultimately God's and therefore the possession of all men.[8] In sum, Judaism advocates justice and equitable distribution of wealth and earthly goods, and not equality of poverty for all.

These concepts, indeed, are archetypal of the modern Israeli concept of practicable idealism, of ethically motivated pragmatism, a blending of what *should* be with what *can* be, given human will and human effort. Throughout history man has indisputably been preoccupied with the acquisition of material goods; and it would appear likely that this preoccupation will not cease in the world as we know it, even if a valid moral or logical case for it could be established. Recognizing the nature of human preoccupations, therefore, traditional Judaism and modern Israel have limited their objectives of reform to humanizing and socializing the drive for material goods and benefits, determined that it be directed toward the benefit of the broadest possible strata of society and that it not be restricted to the gratification of a privileged few.

The Jewish nation has from time immemorial been problem-oriented. It has recognized two things: first, that such problems as we have cited do exist and that no social institution can claim, let alone justifiably pursue, perfection in solving them and, second, that once these problems are identified, society must not ignore them but confront them directly, committed to the most effective means of dealing with them. The history of the Jewish people, from its earliest stages, abounds in examples of frank admission of these problems and the determination to meet them head on. The great prophets were acutely aware of these problems and felt it incumbent on themselves to warn the people of them, to admonish them to stay on the right "road of life," and were therefore known as "prophets of wrath." They were genuine reformers, great initiators of moral and social change, facing up to shallow "modernists" and intractable traditionalists alike with devastating candor and courage. This conflict is, of course, still with us on both fronts. Man will always have with him those who remain dedicated to the achievement of what they consider desirable changes and objectives and those who, almost wholly negatively and pessimistically, are content merely to criticize, to "stand pat," to reconcile present realities with past formulas rather than vice versa.

In the last few years the confrontation has persisted. The central issues have been concern for what some see as a worsening decrease in dedication to national ends, a mounting desire for personal gain, tension between the richer and poorer strata of society, tension between native Israelis and immigrants, and fear in some quarters that the general quality of life in Israel is deteriorating.

Plausible explanations can be given for certain changes in attitude and the problems—real, exaggerated, or imaginary—that face Israel at present. For one, perhaps the continual sacrifices, the unceasing efforts demanded of Israelis in their incessant struggle for their very existence, have taken their understandably human toll, forcing a reaction, a growing wave of individualism, a more marked pursuit of personal as opposed to national aims. The preparation, education, and motivation of the early Israeli pioneers was perhaps more thorough than that of their own offspring or of later immigrants. The dedication and labor that could be expected of these pioneers—this smaller, more intimate group—while the nation was still few in numbers became, in the natural course of events, more difficult to achieve as Israel grew into a larger, more heterogeneous society. Israel's development brought with it, inescapably, problems of congestion, urbanization, ecology, communication, all the attendant challenges of growth. As in other countries the growth of the mass media, including television, has had a great growth on the attitude of Israelis, focusing greater attention on issues of social unrest, strikes, and tension among Israelis coming from different countries, at times forcing a revision of uncritically accepted Israeli norms and institutions. On the more positive side, however, perhaps this very acceleration of mass media communication will force Israelis to pay closer attention to the "smaller" questions of daily life, such as everyday good manners, civility in human relations, order and propriety in public places—once understandably considered "luxuries" among people struggling for their very existence. This might come as a surprise to some Israelis who perhaps have an exaggerated idealistic image of themselves. I believe it merely reflects the simple truth that Israel, because of her unique situation, faces problems of development, both of developed and developing countries.

In 1970-72 several steps were taken to meet these challenges. A special advisor was appointed to promote voluntary action aiming to improve the social fabric of Israel, to achieve national objectives of advancing the general scale of national values, and to affect the nation's general quality of life. An *ad hoc* committee, composed of academicians and professionals, prepared a wide-ranging report on subjects related to youth in distress. The report, focusing on the needs of children and youth, attempted to make specific and general recommendations on how to eliminate poverty, retardation, and underdevelopment among at least a portion of the Israeli population. It was hoped that by confronting these problems boldly, honestly, and imaginatively, Israel might be able not only to help meet its internal problems but also to derive lessons of possible interest and benefit to others.

In summary, then, what is the general message of Israel to other developing nations? To what extent are the fruits of Israel's own experience, gained through experiment, success, failure, and resulting expertise, applicable to these nations?

First, Israel offers the important lesson of optimism and hope, a determination never to give up no matter what the obstacles might be. Israel's very creation and accelerated growth in the face of tremendous adversities, limitations and paucity of its natural resources, and the complexity of its population composition and increase are themselves proofs that even under apparently insurmountable problems successful, even rapid development is feasible if certain conditions are met. Among these conditions perhaps the decisive one is a strong will to persevere, to advance in the task of development no matter what difficulties might be encountered. Another essential condition of success is a high degree of personal identification with national aims and broad participation in developmental projects by all strata of the population. Such participation is possible only when a nation at large consciously strives to achieve social justice, with a genuine, continuing care for the underprivileged. For ultimately a nation can rise no higher than its least fortunate.

Second, Israel's experience, at least, has proven that there is no short road to development. It is an arduous but not an impossible task. Again, it must be said that development requires dedication of a very tangible kind: the individual's identification with national objectives. It requires a genuine transfer of national resources and opportunities to the less privileged, as well as active support and faith among a nation's population at large and among its leaders.

Third, it must always be remembered thst the field of national development is a broad and complex one, with both internal and external implications—already cited in the case of Israel—of surpassing importance. Without massive assistance from abroad, for example, Israel would not have enjoyed the progress it has known. A recent study by David Horowitz analyzes, among other matters, the dynamics of the transfer of capital in the various stages of Israeli development.[9] Horowitz emphasizes that this is only one of the conditions of development, however indispensable. Fortunately, the moral responsibility of richer nations to assist the poorer through a suitable transfer of resources is now widely recognized.

Fourth, the *ethics* of development, as experienced by Israel, points a lesson of both optimism and prudence for others. The rhythm of national development, like the rhythm of nature, involves a sustained interplay of continuity and innovation. Continuity without innovation encourages stagnation and degeneration. Innovation without continuity spells permanent chaos. A synthesis of continuity and innovation, however, assures a rhythm of life and growth. In specific terms of national development, this rhythm presupposes gradual and feasible changes, a continuing interaction between past achievements and plans for future changes. It represents another aspect of the comprehensive approach to development, stressing the need to consider the variety of factors that characterize human society—economic, social, cultural, religious, physical, and ecological. The proper rhythm of development also presupposes the active, sustained involvement of a nation's entire population, especially rural population. those elements of it facing special challenges, notably youth, women, and the rural population.

Israel's experience—at home and in cooperation with developing nations—also forewarns reformers not only that development can be achieved only gradually, step by step, but also that when one set of difficulties has been overcome, another set of challenges emerges. It also would indicate that if a periodic balance of achievement and failure is positive, one should be satisfied that one has done one's best and that one's assets outweigh one's liabilities. Overall successful and useful individual projects should be continued, whether they fit into a total preconceived development strategy or not. This is one point at which the pragmatic should precede the theoretical. We learn, in the sum of things, by doing. Planning is essential; but when plans must be modified, one should have no qualms about modifying them to meet real needs, unembarrassedly, acknowledging the newly discovered need with vigorous readaptation rather than with regret that a theory has been found wanting, even in a minor regard. Indeed, perhaps the most important criterion for planners is the anticipation of such potential changes, the need to plan flexibly, to adjust to evolving conditions. The philosopher Heraclitus assures us that there is nothing permanent in the universe but change. This has certainly been proved true in Israel, where many details in existing plans have been found wanting because overall plans were too rigid and did not allow for adjustments required in the field. Some villages today confront serious problems because plans prepared only 18 years ago did not envisage proper means of caring for grown sons of villagers who wish to become farmers and live in the vicinity of their parental villages.

It would appear that Israel's developmental experience has been of interest and use to other nations basically because it has reflected elements and trends of universal application. Perhaps it is the special conditions that brought about Israel's relatively rapid development that make the nation's experience and conclusions valid for others. Among these conditions has been Israel's traditional insistence on combining the economic and social approaches to development. Obviously, too, Israel's cultural and historical heritage has played a critical role in the formulation of the modalities of its development. In addition Israel, itself suffering from a disruption of certain traditional patterns, has always stressed that local mores and traditions be respected and conserved to the greatest degree possible in every development project.

The very manner in which Israelis discuss difficulties facing them and the way they decide to meet them, again as a problem-oriented society, might also be of interest and inspiration to other developing countries. Israelis have a reputation for frankness in discussing their own problems with strangers—indeed, sometimes to a degree of self-criticism that does not do justice to their achievements. One basis of affinity between Israel and other developing countries has been Israel's candor in admitting that it faces such problems as islands of poverty and social gaps to a greater extent than it anticipated. In addition, Israelis are not characterized by a dogmatic posture. In dialogue they are as anxious to learn as they are to share their experience. One is reminded of an old Talmudic dictum in this context: "I have learned from all my teachers, more from my colleagues, but most from my pupils." In trying to assist others in solving their problems, Israel has realized the scope and impact of its own problems. Genuine assistance *is* dialogue, a two-way process, especially among developing countries confronting comparable challenges.

Israel has participated in projects of development and assistance abroad almost from the time of its creation as an independent state. Its chief motivation has been the desire to participate as fully as possible in what it considers to be one of the most promising and challenging fields of international relations—cooperation in development and assistance. Israel's motivation transcends the economic, the political, the social, even the developmental sphere, however. It has very much to do with a modern and laic application of the time-honored, still cherished belief in the initial and ultimate brotherhood of man.

Such a concept might strike modern ears with less than reverent force. Perhaps two episodes can be cited that will drive home the point of Israel's overriding motivation in cooperating with others.

The story is told that several years ago a visitor to Israel asked his host how Israelis, in view of their massive challenges at home, find the energy, manpower, and will for projects of assistance abroad. The Israeli host recalled the old parable of the two seas fed by the waters of the River Jordan—the Lake of Gennesaret and the Dead Sea. He turned to his guest and asked why the water of the first was sweet and the second salty. His guest did not reply. After a suitable pause the Israeli host explained the parable: The water of the Sea of Galilee is sweet because it both receives and gives water. The water of the Dead Sea is salty and without life because it only receives water and does not give.

An episode in Costa Rica pointed a similar moral. In 1972 a group of Israeli visitors arrived in the village of Naranjo, near San José, to meet the members of the local youth club, the Movimiento Nacional de Juventud. But the visitors arrived late, after the club had concluded its meeting. Only a few of the older members and a group of the youngest remained. The visitors approached those who had remained and asked the oldest, a boy of 12: "Why are you in the movement?" Without hesitation the boy answered: "What a question! We are here so that we can help the community." And the lad listed with pride the various tasks his club had recently fulfilled for the benefit of his community.

The answer of the boy in Naranjo, for all its simplicity, provides perhaps a better insight into the universal truth motivating all those engaged in international development than a library of learned treatises. In its quiet way it reflects the optimism, the faith, the self-reliance, and the need for mutual cooperation and interaction that provide the motivation and inspiration, the very conditions of development cooperation. Without faith, without optimism in the face of any challenge, without self-reliance and cooperation, without social interaction and sharing, not only development projects fail. Man fails.

Jerusalem, September 1973

NOTES

1. Deuteronomy 30:12-14.
2. *The Union Prayerbook for Jewish Worship* (rev. ed.; New York: Central Conference of American Rabbis, 1961), p. 34.
3. Joseph H. Hertz, ed., *Sayings of the Fathers* (New York: Behrman House, 1945), p. 45.
4. *T. Sukkah* 49b. Isidore Epstein, *Judaism* (Baltimore: Penguin Books, 1964), p. 151.
5. Quoted in H. W. Bialik and Y. Ravnizky, *Sefer Ha'agada*, III (Tel Aviv: Dvir, 1936), p. 34. (In Hebrew.)
6. Leviticus 19:15.
7. Deuteronomy 24:13.
8. *T. Babba Kamma*, 81b.
9. D. Horowitz, *Enigma of Economic Growth* (New York: Praeger, 1972).

ISRAEL'S DISBURSEMENTS
ON BILATERAL COOPERATION ACTIVITIES, 1961-71
($ U.S.)

Year	Amount
1961	2,806,000
1962	4,380,000
1963	5,285,000
1964	4,115,000
1965	6,030,000
1966	3,914,000
1967	6,370,000
1968	5,470,000
1969	5,495,000
1970	6,247,000
1971	6,861,000

Notes: 1. The figures represent net disbursements for official bilateral cooperation activities. Overhead expenses such as staff salaries at headquarters, office expenses, and communications are not included. Figures for other official flows, such as contributions to multilateral agencies, are included separately in the budget of the Ministry for Foreign Affairs. Other official flows, such as participation in equity capital or guarantee of investments, are shown in the budget of the Ministry of Finance.

2. The financial year in Israel starts on April 1; therefore the first figure refers to April 1, 1961-March 31, 1962—, and so on.

3. It might be assumed that marked variations between consecutive years represent technicalities of payments and accounting, such as deferred payment, rather than actual difference in scope of activities.

Source: Division of International Cooperation, 1973.

ISRAELI EXPERTS ABROAD
ON BILATERAL PROJECTS, 1958-71

| | By Sector | | |
	1958-65	1966-71	Total
Agriculture	413	1,144	1,557
Cooperatives and labor	21	82	103
Industry and construction	122	139	261
Medicine and public health	183	223	406
Community development and education	121	290	411
Science and technology	—	69	69
Administration	77	175	252
Youth	219	529	748
Various	342	192	534
Total			4,341

| | By Continent | | |
	1958-65	1966-71	Total
Africa	1,078	1,685	2,763
Asia	154	334	488
Mediterranean	159	288	447
Latin America	107	536	643
Total			4,341

Note: The figures refer to experts who served abroad, on both long- and short-term assignments. They represent a cumulative addition of data on the basis of yearly computation.

Source: Division of International Cooperation, 1973.

FOREIGN TRAINEES IN ISRAEL, 1958-71

| By Sector | | |
1958-65	1966-71	Total
Agriculture	3,437	2,625	6,062
Cooperatives and labor	1,526	1,669	3,195
Industry and construction	229	117	346
Medicine and public health	283	623	906
Community development and education	258	1,216	1,474
Science and technology	298	582	880
Administration	150	263	413
Youth	672	354	1,026
Various	615	341	956
Total			15,258

| By Continent | | |
1958-65	1966-71	Total
Africa	3,552	3,245	6,797
Asia	946	1,923	2,869
Mediterranean	1,918	1,151	3,069
Latin America	1,052	1,471	2,523
Total			15,258

Note: The figures refer to trainees who came to Israel to attend courses, study tours, and seminars, or for individual studies, of various duration, organized, assisted or with other forms of official participation of the Division of International Cooperation. They do not include students or research fellows invited directly by academic or other institutions, without participation of the Division. The figures represent a cumulative addition of data on the basis of yearly computation.

Source: Division of International Cooperation, 1973.

ISRAELI EXPERTS ON LONG-TERM
AND SHORT-TERM ASSIGNMENT, 1972

| | Long-Term Assignments | | | |
	Africa	Asia and the Mediter- ranean Area	Latin America	Total
Number of experts	139	22	68	229
Man-years	107.50	16.50	50.75	174.75
Percentage of man- years (continents)	61	10	29	100
Agriculture	31	13.25	37.25	81.50
Rural society and regional planning	—	—	—	—
Cooperative and labor	1	—	1	2
Industry construction and services	2.75	—	—	2.75
Science and technology	5.75	2.25	—	8
Administration and public service	13.25	—	1	14.25
Community development and education	—	—	—	—
Medical and public health	9.75	—	—	9.75
Youth	44	1	11.50	56.50

(continued)

97

	Short-Term Assignments			
	Africa	Asia and the Mediter- ranean Area	Latin America	Total
Number of experts	115	87	110	312
Man-years				
Percentage of man- years (continents)	37	28	35	100
Agriculture	49	64	44	157
Rural society and regional planning	—	7	12	19
Cooperatives and labor	—	—	19	19
Industry construction and services	2	2	11	15
Science and technology	9	6	20	35
Administration and public service	18	3	1	22
Community development and education	12	2	1	15
Medical and public health	17	2	1	20
Youth	8	1	1	10

Source: Division of International Cooperation, 1973.

FOREIGN TRAINEES IN ISRAEL, 1972

	Africa	Asia and the Mediterranean Area	Latin America	Total
Agriculture	105	119	24	248
Rural society and regional planning	13	30	10	53
Cooperatives and labor	80	87	41	208
Science and technology	48	52	34	134
Administration and public services	38	25	42	105
Community development and education	85	117	1	203
Medicine and public health	27	12	52	91
Youth	6	4	42	52
Total	402	446	246	1,094

Source: Division of International Cooperation, 1973.

ISRAEL'S COOPERATION PROJECTS, 1972

	Africa	Asia and the Mediterranean Area	Latin America	Total
Number of countries	28	10	19	57
Number of projects	67	12	35	114
Agriculture	23	7	22	52
Rural society and regional planning	—	—	1	1
Cooperatives and labor	1	—	1	2
Industry construction and services	4	—	—	4
Science and technology	8	3	2	13
Administration and public services	7	—	1	8
Community development and education	1	—	1	2
Medicine and public health	10	2	—	12
Youth	13	—	7	20

Source: Department of International Cooperation, 1973.

ISRAEL'S FOREIGN AGRICULTURAL PROJECTS, 1972

	Africa	Asia and the Mediterranean Area	Latin America
Number of projects	23	7	22
Specialized projects	10	1	10
Farms (observation, demonstration, experimentation)	6	3	1
Development—rural institutions in existing villages	4	1	3
Comprehensive regional projects	3	2	8

Source: Division of International Cooperation, 1973.

ISRAEL'S FOREIGN YOUTH PROJECTS, 1972

Activity	Africa (13)	Latin America (7)	Totals (20)
National service, training and settlements	Ivory Coast, Dahomey	Ecuador, Colombia	4
Agricultural training to soldiers	—	Bolivia	1
National youth movement—mainly rural and in agriculture	Malawi, Swaziland, Cameroun, * Togo, Chad**	—	5
National youth movement—mainly educational	Liberia, Niger**	Costa Rica, Panama, El Salvador, Venezuela	6
National youth movement—education and vocational training	Rwanda, Gabon, Lesotho	—	3
Specialized programs	Senegal	—	1

*An additional project is the Centre for the Training of Youth Leaders.
**Discontinued, after rupture of diplomatic relations.
Source: Division of International Cooperation, 1973.

SELECTED PROJECTS ABROAD, 1972

Latin America

Argentina   Preliminary work for establishment of a regional institute for research on arid zones
Preparation of a Latin American seminar on prevention of water contamination
Agreement on agricultural research

Barbados   Agricultural marketing
Port development

Bolivia   Seven agricultural farms of the Engineer Corps
Survey for irrigation projects in the Altiplano

Brazil   Six pilot settlement projects in the Northeast
Preparatory work for an agreement on scientific cooperation
Course on regional comprehensive planning in Fortaleza
Study on spatial directions in development projects of the Northeast

Chile   Irrigation projects, implementation, methods, and training in optimal utilization of water
Scientific cooperation with two universities on arid zones
Course on agricultural extension

Colombia   Preparation for a Latin American course on food technology in 1973
Advisory services on agricultural settlement and training to the armed forces
Establishment of a department for training in rural cooperatives in SENA, the National Institute for Vocational Training

Costa Rica	Youth movement
	Training in agriculture at the National Institute for Vocational Training
Dominican Republic	El Sisal scheme of comprehensive regional settlement in the Azua Valley
	Agricultural marketing
Ecuador	Advisory services in activities of the Institute for Agrarian Reform and Colonization and the Agricultural Military Service
	Preparations for establishment of a workers' bank
El Salvador	Cotton farms
	Youth movement
Guatemala	Cultivation of vegetables in cooperatives, irrigation
	Central American seminar on youth leadership
Guyana	Citriculture and subtropical fruits
Haiti	Agreement on intensification of technical cooperation
	Training in irrigation methods and agricultural techniques, planning for additional cooperatives, crops for export
Honduras	Preparation for course in cooperative transport
Jamaica	Course on rural cooperatives
Mexico	Agreement and implementation of projects in scientific cooperation (mainly irrigation, desalinization)
	Agreement on training of middle-level personnel
Nicaragua	Advisory services in the Rigoberto Cabezas regional scheme
	Survey on possibilities of resettlement following the earthquake in Managua
Panama	Youth movement
	Advisory services in irrigation project of Río Hato
Paraguay	Project of supervised credit in several villages

Peru	Settlement schemes (La Joya, La Yarada), irrigation methods, marketing, field crops
	Cooperative transport Preparation for regional institute for research on arid zones
Trinida and Tobago	Advisory service in agricultural credits, marketing, cattle breeding
Uruguay	Follow-up on 1971 study on citrus development and rehabilitation Report on agroindustrial project in Artigas
Venezuela	New agreement with the National Office for the Coordination of Development and Planning on Advisory Services, on advisory services in agriculture, colonization, organization of cooperatives, agricultural mechanization, and training Youth movement

Asia

Iran	Poultry farming Laboratory for soil mechanics Ghazvin region (carried out by TAHAL)
Khmer Republic	Development scheme in Prek Thnot Valley—extension services, new varieties of rice and sorghum, optimization of water utilization
Laos	Development scheme at Nam Ngum, on the Vientiane Plains—new crops, extension services, multipurpose producer cooperatives
Nepal	Agricultural settlement schemes in the Nawalpur and Nepalganj regions Introduction of cotton
Philippines	Barrio Ricarte model village, in the Nueva Ecija region—organization of multipurpose producer cooperative Courses on use of fertilizers and extension methods

Thailand	Institute for educational aids in vocational training
	Advisory services in agriculture
	Preparation of a course on water resources in 1973 (in cooperation with the U.N. Economic Commission for Asia and the Far East)

Africa

Botswana	Consultants to Ministry of Health in campaign against tuberculosis
	Geological survey for development of potash exploitation
Burundi	Survey for proposed establishment of a training farm at the School of Agriculture in Bujumbura, the capital
Cameroun	Instruction at the National Institute of Youth and Sport
	Advisory services in agricultural settlements, rural youth center, vegetable growing, and marketing
Chad	Afforestation project of 2,000 hectares
	Government printing office
	Agricultural farm and youth training
	(Projects in Chad discontinued after break in diplomatic relations)
Dahomey	Pioneer Youth
	Model citrus and mixed farm, extension activities
Ethiopia	Blood bank
	Geological survey
	Training of hotel personnel
	Advisory services in port development and in fisheries
	Teaching and research project in microbiology, at Haile Selassie University, Addis Ababa
Gabon	National Youth Service and youth program in schools
Gambia	Advisory services to the Ministry of Agriculture
	Courses on extension methods

Ghana	Four state cattle farms, experimentation, and introduction of new crops
Ivory Coast	Advisory services to Service Civique (National Youth Service) at Central Training Base in Bouaké and in regional districts Rural extension Marketing of tropical fruits
Kenya	Research in agriculture Teaching in the university Operations research in services for outpatients
Lesotho	Youth service, training in agriculture and village skills, and general education
Liberia	Agreement on establishment of a company for operation of agricultural machinery
Madagascar	Major citrus project Agricultural training center
Malawi	Young Pioneer Movement, central training school and district centers; agricultural plans for graduates Ophthalmology Courses on extension methods
Mali	Survey on establishment of national lottery Fieldwork of participants in Mount Carmel course for kindergarten teachers (Projects discontinued after break in diplomatic relations)
Niger	Training in agriculture Youth movement Medical survey (Projects discontinued after break in diplomatic relations)
Nigeria	Survey on use of computers Survey on poultry farming Preparations for training of kindergarten teachers
Rwanda	Youth movement School for medical assistants

Senegal	Survey for development of tourism Youth service
Swaziland	Youth movement
Sierra Leone	Citriculture, irrigation
Togo	Youth service
Uganda	Citrus project Advisory services to Ministry of Finance Advisory services on use of computors Teaching at Makarere University (Projects discontinued after break in diplomatic relations during 1971)
Upper Volta	Agricultural training center at Matourku Forestry Medicine (pediatrics)
Zaïre	Medicine (pediatrics) Advisory services in hospital administration and medical training
Zambia	Comprehensive agricultural plans in Kafubu and Kafulafuta regions Planning for new comprehensive projects

Source: Division of International Cooperation, 1973.

MAIN COURSES, SEMINARS, AND STUDY TOURS
HELD IN ISRAEL, 1972

Subject	Institution	Duration (months)	Participants
Public health, social medicine	H.U. Hadassah School of Medicine	14	9
Groundwater exploration	Hebrew University (H.U.)	6	11
Comprehensive regional planning	Settlement Study Centre	12	25
Farm Management	Ministry of Agriculture, Foreign Training Department (M.A.F.T.D.)	6	27
Basic medical sciences (teacher training)	H.U. Hadassah School of Medicine	12	4
Agricultural meteorology	Israel Meteorological Service	3.5	14
Cooperative transport	Cooperative Studies Centre for Latin America	2.5	21
Cooperation and labor studies	International Institute for Cooperative and Labour Studies (I.I.C.L.S.)	3.5	52
Food and applied nutrition	Mt. Carmel Centre	6	23
Nursery and kindergarten teaching	Mt. Carmel Centre	6	19
Industrial management	Cooperative Studies Centre for Latin America	2	18
Fruit orchards	M.A.F.T.D.	1	20

(continued)

109

Subject	Institution	Duration (months)	Participants
Cooperation and labor studies	I.I.C.L.S.	2.5	43
Water resources management	Technion (Israel Institute of Technology)	2.5	11
Cooperative bookkeeping	Cooperative Studies Centre for Latin America	2	22
Cooperatives in Israel (for members of the Co-operative College, Paris)	I.I.C.L.S.	0.5	12
Poultry husbandry and extension	M.A.F.T.D.	4	19
Agricultural extension	M.A.F.T.D.	4	22
Comprehensive regional planning	Settlement Study Centre	12	24
Functional literacy in youth programs	Mt.Carmel Centre	2.5	15
Sources of employment	Cooperative Studies Centre for Latin America	0.5	9
Financing of urban development	Cooperative Studies Centre for Latin America	1.5	25
Rural community development	Mt.Carmel Centre	6	23
Data processing	Institute of Productivity	0.5	20
Cooperation and labor studies	I.I.C.L.S.	2.5	55
Rural health services	Sick Fund, Histadrut (General Federation of Labour)	2	24
Public health and Social medicine	H.U. Hadassah School of Medicine	14	16

Subject	Institution	Duration (months)	Participants
Kindergarten teachers and supervisors	Mt. Carmel Centre	8.5	20
Groundwater exploration	H.U.	5	26
Farm management	M.A.F.T.D.	5	19
Youth leadership	M.A.F.T.D.	1.5	43
Agricultural meteorology	Institute of Meteorology, Ministry of Transport	3.5	18
Home economics extension (study tour)	Mt. Carmel Centre	0.5	12

Source: Division of International Cooperation, 1973.

LOCAL COURSES AND SEMINARS HELD ABROAD, 1972

Selected List by Countries

Country	Subject
Barbados	Rural cooperation
Brazil1	Comprehensive regional planning
Chile	Agricultural extension methods
Costa Rica	Agricultural cooperatives, youth leadership
Cyprus	Agricultural meteorology
El Salvador	Youth leadership
Gambia	Agricultural extension, extension methods
Guatemala	Youth leadership
Jamaica	Rural cooperation
Khmer Republic	Agricultural extension (2)
Korea	Extension methods, fertilizer use
Laos	Extension methods, rural cooperatives
Malawi	Extension methods (2)
Nicaragua	Agricultural cooperation
Panama	Youth leadership
Peru	Extension Methods
Philippines	Fertilizer use, extension methods (3)
Thailand	Fertilizer use, extension methods
Togo	Hotel management (2)
Turkey	Plant genetics

By Sectors and Continents

Course	Africa	Asia	Latin America	Total
Agriculture	3	10	2	15
Regional planning	—	—	1	1
Management and administration	7	2	—	9
Youth	—	—	4	4
Cooperation	—	—	4	4
Total	10	12	11	33

Note: In 1972 more than 1,000 students participated in local courses and seminars organized by Israeli agencies and institutions.

Source: Division of International Cooperation, 1973.

COUNTRIES WITH WHICH ISRAEL HAS SIGNED

COOPERATION AGREEMENTS

Bolivia	1961, 1972	Liberia	1962
Brazil	1962, 1973	Malagasy Republic	1964
Burundi	1962	Mali	1969
Cameroun	1962	Mexico	1966, 1973
Central African		Nicaragua	1966
Republic	1962	Niger	1963
Chad	1964	Panama	1970
Chile	1965	Peru	1963
Colombia	1965	Philippines	1964
Costa Rica	1965, 1971	Rumania	1967
Dahomey	1961	Rwanda	1962
Dominican Republic	1963	Sierra Leone	1965
El Salvador	1971	Tanzania	1963
Gabon	1962	Togo	1964
Ghana	1962, 1973	Turkey	1964
Guatemala	1971	Uganda	1963
Haiti	1972	Upper Volta	1961
Honduras	1967	Uruguay	1968
Ivory Coast	1962	Venezuela	1966
Kenya	1966	Zaïre	1964

Source: Division of International Cooperation.

113

SELECTED LIST OF PUBLICATIONS, 1972

Many Israeli professional and executive agencies annually prepare reports and studies on development problems in their respective fields. Following is a selection of reports and studies produced in 1972.

Agriculture
(published by the Centre for International Agricultural Cooperation)

1. M. Zur, Cotton Growing in Newalpur and Nepalganj Projects; a Summary of Field Trials in 1971 and Experiments Proposed for 1972.

2. Y. Yagel, Hydroponic Vegetable Growing in Singapore (Nov. 1969-Sept. 1971); a Report on Various Hydroponic Vegetable Trials.

3. N. Kedar, Advancement of Vegetable Growing in Cooperative Development Projects in Tropical Countries.

4. E. Golan, Report on a Survey of Citrus Groves in Malta (15-20.3.72).

5. K. Mendel and M. Bar-Lev, Israel's Agricultural Research Programmes in Joint Rural Development Projects; Annual Report 1970-1971, on sorghum, groundnuts, vegetables, corn.

6. G. Tabor, Draft Proposals for the Establishment of an Extension Framework and Training Program for Agricultural Personnel in the Lower Mekong Basin.

7. Yehuda Orshan and Yitzhak Remer, Acuerdo OEA-Israel, Informe de la misión de estudio de prefactibilidad del proyecto regional agro-industrial Colonia E. Acevedo en el Dept. Artigas. . . Uruguay.

8. Ari Lahav, Proyecto El Sisal—etapa C, República Dominicana; el sistema de riego y agua potable, y la planificación física.

9. Shlomo Zamir, Proyecto Caldeirão, Brazil; proyecto de drenagem superficial e sub-superficial.

10. R. Moshe, I. Rapport de reconnaissance des sols du projet de plantation d'agrumes de Morandava; S. Marish, II. Etude des sols et problemes de drainage du projet de plantation d'agrumes de Morandava.

11. Kingdom of Thailand, Ministry of National Development, Hup-Kapong; a Thai-Israeli Joint Venture in Rural Development, Summary of Five Years of Cooperation, 1966-1971.

12. A. Blum, Promotion of Sorghum Growing in Various Projects in the Tropics; a Report of a Mission and Résumé of Field Trials for 1971/72. (Hebrew.)

Mount Carmel International Training Centre for Community Services
(1971, 1972)

Reports on

1. Course for nursery and kindergarten teachers
   January 5 - July 5, 1971   Hebrew and English

2. Study tour on program for the education of adults
   February - March 1971   English and Hebrew
   Participants from African and Asian countries were education officers engaged in planning, administration, and supervision; teachers; and community development officers. The study tour observed and analyzed education programs in Israel for youths and adults ranging from literacy classes to university extension courses.

3. Symposium on the changing needs of women's education in the Second Development Decade.
   April 2-9, 1971   English and French
   The symposium was attended by participants from 20 countries (Africa, Latin America, Asia) each of whom had attended one of the seven seminars held during the decade 1961-71.

4. Course on social welfare services — functions and methods
   June 15 - September 15, 1971   English and Hebrew
   Papers prepared by students:
   ● The main social problems in four East African countries
   ● Social problems in three West African countries
   ● Social problems in three Asian countries
   ● Four papers presented by Miss Emily A. Senalor, Dept. of Social Welfare and Community Development, Accra, Ghana

5. Study tour on consumer education and cooperation within the framework of community development
   July 15 - September 15, 1971   English and Hebrew

6. Tournée d'etudes sur les programmes d'éducation pour adultes
   October 20 - December 1, 1971
   Similar to course No. 2.

7. Course on food and applied nutrition
   January 10 - July 10, 1972   English
   In cooperation with FAO.
   Appendix 3   Selection of assignments
   Appendix 4   Final group assignment, improvement plan
                  written in Zambia
   Fieldwork in Zambia, May 26 - July 10, 1972, by Miss B. E. Van Dam, FAO nutrition officer.

8. Stage de formation de jardinières d'enfants
   January 5 - July 5, 1972

9. Course on functional literacy in the framework of youth programs
   July 17 - September 30, 1972

10. Study tour for home extension officers
    October 5-19, 1972

11. Educational Aspects in Developing Countries With Emphasis on Adult Literacy, by Margot Lifmann, 1972.

Centre for Cooperation and Labour Studies for Latin America
H. Halperin, Agrindus

Afro-Asian Institute for Cooperative and Labour Studies

1. A. Eger, Israel and the Emerging Nations.

2. A. Szeskin, The World Cooperative Movement.

The Settlement Study Centre

1. Y. Ginsberg, The Rural-Urban Migration in Israel.

2. Y. Cotten, The Influence of Urban Zones in the Southern Coastal Plan of Israel.

116

3. D. Weitz, The Spatial Organization of Rural Development.

4. E. Cohen and E. Leshem, Survey of Rural Cooperation in Three Regions of Collective Settlements.

5. The Regional Cooperation in Israel—Publications of Problems of Regional Development.

Note: The publications listed in this appendix can be obtained from the institutions that published them.

ISRAELI EXPERTS WITH INTERNATIONAL
ORGANIZATIONS IN DEVELOPING COUNTRIES, 1972

| | Long-Term Assignments | | | | Assignments at Head-quarters |
	Africa	Asia and the Mediterranean	Latin America	Total	
FAO	7	6	5	18	4
IAEA	—	—	—	—	2
ILO	3	8	5	16	—
WHO	8	3	2	13	8
ORT	3	—	—	3	—
UN	7	4	5	16	12
UNIDO	3	1	5	9	2
UNESCO	6	3	2	11	1
WMO	—	—	1	1	—
ECA	2	—	—	2	—
ECLA	—	—	1	1	—
UNHCR	1	—	—	1	1
ITU	1	—	—	1	—
IMF	2	—	1	3	12
IBRD	—	1	—	1	—
ISVS	—	1	2	3	—
UNCTAD	—	1	—	1	1
UNDP	—	1	—	1	1
UNICEF	1	—	—	1	—

Totals:
Short-term assignments: 60
Long-term assignments: 102
Headquarters assignments: 47
209

Source: Division of International Cooperation, 1973.

ORGANIZATION OF ISRAEL'S COOPERATION PROJECTS

The Division of International Cooperation is the largest unit in the Ministry for Foreign Affairs. The director reports to the assistant director-general in charge of international cooperation and economic affairs. The Division is responsible for identification, budgeting, supervision, and evaluation of official cooperation projects.

The director of the Division is assisted by deputies and chiefs of sections. Geographical sections maintain contact with embassies abroad and with area officers at headquarters and foreign embassies in Israel, in order to identify the optimal cooperation projects according to needs and requests of receiving countries. Operational sections in charge of training, manpower, and budget maintain contact with professional and executive agencies in Israel in order to identify, select, and supervise execution of optimal cooperation projects according to Israel's ability to provide.

Additional sections in the Division are International Organizations, Publications, Reporting, and Evaluation.

The actual projects abroad and at home are carried out by professional and executive agencies, both official and private.

The main professional and executive agencies involved in official cooperation projects in 1972 are the following:

International Agricultural Cooperation Centre, Ministry of Agriculture
Foreign Training Department, Ministry of Agriculture
Water Resources Commission, Ministry of Agriculture
Ministry of Education
Consultant for Medical Cooperation, Ministry of Health
National Council for Research and Development, Prime Minister's
    Office
Traffic Department, Ministry of Police
Office Mechanization Centre, Ministry of Finance
Department for Local Government, Ministry of Interior
Foreign Trade Department, Ministry for Commerce and Industry
Meteorological Service, Ministry of Transport
Ministry for Social Welfare
Institute of Productivity
Histadrut, Department for Foreign Relations
Afro-Asian Institute for Cooperative and Labour Studies

Centre for Cooperation and Labour Studies for Latin America
Mt. Carmel International Training Centre for Community Services
Volcani Institute for Agricultural Research
Negev Institute for Arid Zones Research
Department for Vocational Training, Ministry of Labour
Department for Audiovisual Aids, Ministry of Labour
Hadassah Medical School, Hebrew University
    Department of Microbiology
    Department of Public Health
    Department of Ophthalmology
Harry S. Truman Research Institute for Developing Countries,
    Hebrew University
Groundwater Research Centre, Hebrew University
Central Sick Fund, Histadrut
Technion
Fertilizers and Chemical Development Council, Ministry of
    Development
Settlement Study Centre, Rehovot

Source: Division for International Cooperation.

ISRAEL'S TRADE AND ECONOMIC ACTIVITIES, 1972

Activity	Africa	Asia	Latin America	Total
1. Approved investments in joint ventures ($U.S.)[a]	8,107,000	1,138,000	100,000	9,345,000
2. Number of joint ventures:				
Industry	13	6	1	20
Agriculture	2	1	—	3
Services	5	1	—	6
Total	20	8	1	29
3. Volume of work executed by Israeli firms ($U.S.)				
Building and construction	45,000,000	17,554,000	5,800,000	68,354,000
Planning and consulting	2,691,000	1,410,000	1,171,000	5,272,000
Total	47,691,000	18,964,000	6,971,000	73,626,000
4. Exports ($U.S.)	36,700,000[b]	141,600,000[c]	14,200,000	192,500,000
5. Imports ($U.S.)	20,300,000[b]	10,700,000[c]	34,900,000	65,900,000

[a]In share capital, proprietors, loans, and guarantees.
[b]Excluding South Africa.
[c]Excluding Japan.

Source: Ministry of Finance, Foreign Exchange Department, 1973.

Bilateral projects: Projects agreed upon between Israel and the receiving country

Capital cooperation: Transfer of flows through grants or concessionary loans, in untied capital or in goods and services

Comprehensive regional planning: Planning of regions on the subnational level, combining social and economic aspects of both urban and rural population in agriculture, industry, and services; accepted in Israel since early 1950s

Development cooperation: Programs of development jointly decided upon between donor and receiving countries; in the 1950s referred to as development assistance

Gadna: Abbreviation of *Gedudey Noar* (Youth Battalions), a premilitary organization for training youth between the ages of 14 and 18

Histadrut: Accepted short name for *Histadrut Haovdim Hakelalit* (General Federation of Labor), Israel's largest labor organization

Kibbutz: Agricultural collective settlement; the first, Deganta Alef, was established in 1909

Knesset: Parliament of Israel

Local courses: Held in receiving countries, conducted with the help of local experts and those sent from Israel; also referred to as "mobile courses" because experts sent from Israel conduct more than one course abroad

Moshav: Agricultural cooperative village or multipurpose agricultural cooperative; the first, Nahalal, was established in 1921

Multilateral projects: Agreed upon between Israel, the receiving country, and one or more partners, usually another country or an international development agency

Nahal: Abbreviation of *Noar Halutz Lohem* (Fighting Pioneering Youth), army service combining agricultural work and military training

Rehovot movement: International conferences held every two years in Rehovot, seat of the Weizmann Institute of Science, dedicated to discussion of development programs with joint participation of policy-makers and scientists

Rural center: Center serving several villages and offering such services as a school, a medical center, a supermarket, and a depot for heavy machinery

Solel Boneh: In Hebrew, Paver and Builder; big construction company of the *Histadrut*

Supervised credit: Agricultural revolving credit, mainly in the form of producer goods and services, usually supervised by committees composed of representatives of the cooperative, the bank, and the extension service

TAHAL: In Hebrew, *Tihnun Hamaim Le'Israel* (Water Planning for Israel), the main water planning and consulting firm in Israel

Technical cooperation: Mainly projects aimed at transfer of skills, training of local manpower, or temporary fulfillment of operational functions; main methods are the sending of experts and receiving of students and trainees.

Youth *Aliya*:   (Youth immigration), an organization that received and educated tens of thousands of children and youth, who often arrived in Israel without their parents, since the ascent of the Nazi regime in Germany; it combined work, usually in agricultural settlements and schools, with vocational training and general education

Zionism: Jewish national movement started in the nineteenth century, aimed at gathering the Jews to the country of their forefathers (from Zion, one of the mountains of Jerusalem)

Horowitz, David. *The Enigma of Economic Growth—A Case Study of Israel.* New York: Praeger, 1972.

Kreinin, Mordechai E. *Israel and Africa—A Case Study in Technical Cooperation.* New York: Praeger, 1964.

Laufer, Leopold. *Israel and the Developing Countries, New Approaches to Cooperation.* New York: The Twentieth Century Fund, 1967.

Macarow, David, and Gershon Fradkin. *The Short Course in Development Training.* Ramat Gan: Massada, 1973.

Ministry for Foreign Affairs, Division of International Cooperation. *Israel's Programme of International Cooperation.* Jerusalem: the Ministry, 1971.

Ministry for Foreign Affairs, Division of International Cooperation, and Ministry of Agriculture, Centre for Agricultural Cooperation. *Israel's Agricultural Cooperation with Developing Countries, Concepts—Objectives—Projects.* Jerusalem: the Ministries, 1971.

Tal, Eliezer, and Yaron Ezrahi, eds. *Science Policy and Development, the Case of Israel—Israel-American Symposium on Science Policy and Organization of Research—1970.* New York and London: Gordon and Breach Science, 1972.

Truman Research Institute. *Technical Assistance and Development, Proceedings of International Conference, 1970.* Jerusalem: the Hebrew University, 1971.

Weisner, Stan. *Professional Social Work in Kenya—Training and Performance.* A critical evaluation of the former Kenya-Israel School of Social Work. Nairobi: Office of the President of Kenya and Embassy of Israel, 1972.

Weitz, Raanan. *From Peasant to Farmer—a Revolutionary Strategy for Development.* New York and London: Columbia University Press, 1971.

Weitz, Raanan, and Avshalom Rokach. *Agricultural Development, Planning and Implementation (Israel Case Study).* Dordrecht: D. Reidel, 1968.

Wiener, Aaron. *The Role of Water in Development—an Analysis of Principles of Comprehensive Planning.* New York: McGraw-Hill, 1972.

Yalan, Emmanuel, et al. *The Modernization of Traditional Agricultural Villages—Minority Villages in Israel.* Rehovot: Settlement Study Centre: 1972.

Federal University of Ceará,
Brazil, 26
Federman Company, 84
field projects, 62, 63
Finca-escuela, 19-20, 32-33
firms, private sector, 25-26, 28,
78-85
Food and Agricultural Organiza-
tion (FAO), 30, 40, 70, 83
Foundation for Training and Applied
Research of the Agrarian Reform
(see CIARA)
Friedrich Ebert Foundation, 49
Fritz Naphtali Foundation, 51
Fundación para Capacitación y In-
vestigación Applicada de la Re-
forma Agraria (see CIARA)

Gadna, 38, 39, 41
Galbraith, John K., 46
Gambia, 67
General Federation of Labor (see
Histadrut)
Ghana, 3, 19, 72, 80, 83, 84-85
Ghazvin, Iran, 28, 30-31, 82
Gordon, Aharon David, 13
Great Britain, 2, 49
Greece, 34, 74
Guatemala, 51
Guinea, 73

Hacohen, David, 2, 3
Hagana, 48
Haifa University, 45
Haile Selassie I University of Addis
Ababa, 54
Hebrew University, 55; Department
of African Studies, 65; Department
of Microbiology, 65
Hebrew University Hadassah Medical
School (HUHMS), 58; Department
of Opthalmology, 59
Heraclitus, 91
Histadrut, 2, 48, 52, 79, 80, 84; In-
ternational Department, 48
Honduras, 51

Horowitz, David, 91
HUHMS (see Hebrew University
Hadassah Medical School)
human resources: development, 9,
12, 22, 53-60; in planning, 14
human technology, 11, 27

IAN (see Instituto Agrario Nacional)
ideology, 2, 9-10, 13, 38, 86-93
ILO (see International Labour Organization)
immigration, 1, 9, 10, 12, 13, 14-15,
79, 89; Second Aliya, 13, 46
"implementationism," 2-3
implementation, of project, 6, 14,
24, 28-29, 34, 50, 62, 63, 70
India, 74
industry, 13, 14, 34, 48, 84-85 (see
also urban sector)
Institute for Planning and Development (IPD), 85
institutions: economic and social,
17, 21; establishment of, 7, 8, 11,
25, 28-29, 63; support, 65 (see
also cooperatives; research institutions; rural institutions;
training, institutions)
Instituto Agrario Nacional (IAN),
22, 23, 24 (see also Venezuela)
integrated project, 68-69
Inter-American Development Bank,
7, 21, 22, 25, 30, 52, 62, 75
International Bank for Reconstruction and Development (see World
Bank)
International Cell Research Organization, 55
International Labour Organization
(ILO), 6, 51, 70
International Trade Union Congress,
Belgrade, 3
Iran, 28, 30-31, 45, 74, 82, 83; Plan
Organization, 83
International Youth Cooperation
Centre, 76
irrigation (see water, irrigation)

128

methodology, development, 5-8, 12,
33; assistance, 69-70; experts,
63-65; modernization, 15-16;
planning, 62; problems of, 61-70
Mexico, 55; Council for Science
and Technology, 56
Michaelson, Isaac, 59
microbiology, 54-55, 63, 65
Middle East, 74, 79, 80, 82, 83
Mikveh, Israel, 12
military, 28-29, 38-40 (see also
Gadna; Nahal)
Ministry for Foreign Affairs, 26,
72, 75; Israel Association for
International Cooperation, 76
(see also Division for International Cooperation)
Ministry of Agriculture, 15, 26, 68;
Foreign Training Department,
67, 69, 76; International Agricultural Cooperation Centre, 27, 56,
76; Irrigation and Drainage Department, 83; Planning Department, 54
Ministry of Defense, 37; Department
of International Cooperation, 37-
38 (see also International Youth
Cooperation Centre)
Ministry of Finance, controller of
foreign exchange, 78, 79
Ministry of Housing, 26
Ministry of Interior, 26
Ministry of Labour, 26
minorities, Israel, 15-16
modernization, 67; agriculture, 11,
14, 20, 21, 22, 30-34; of Israel's
minorities, 15-16; methodology,
15-16; of villages, 15-16, 17, 26,
28
moshav, 13, 14, 30, 46-47, 64 (see
collectives; communes; cooperatives; kibbutz)
Moslems, 15
motivation: Israel's, 1-4, 92-93
(see also cooperation projects;
Israel, experience as a develop-

ing country)
Motoragri, 84
Mount Carmel International Training Centre for Community Services (MCTC), 43-45, 69, 76
Movimiento Nacional de Juventud,
92
multilateral assistance (see assistance, multilateral)
multilateral projects, 6-7, 69-70
multiplier effect, 20, 23, 25, 55, 58,
63, 68

Nabatean agriculture, 15
Nahal, 38-40
Nairobi, 45, 70
Nam-Ngum, Laos, 33
Naranjo, Costa Rica, 92
National Agrarian Institute (see
Instituto Agrario Nacional)
National Council for Research and
Development, 15, 56, 59
National Institute for Cooperatives,
Peru, 51
National Water Carrier, 80, 82, 83
Nepal, 72
Netherlands, the, 70; Dutch
Agency for International Coopera-
tion, 70
Netter, Karl, 12
Niger, 74
Nigeria, 45, 82, 83

OAS (see Organization of American
States)
OECD (see Organization for Economic
Cooperation and Development)
Organization for Economic Coopera-
tion and Development (OECD), 34,
54; Development Assistance Com-
mittee, 3, 61
Organization of American States
(OAS), 7, 22, 51, 55, 59, 63, 73, 75

Palestine, 37
Parliament of Israel (see Knesset)

Peru, 45, 51, 55, 69, 82
pest control (see cotton cultivation)
Petrolandia, 19-21, 25
phasing out, 63-64 (see also experts, phasing out)
Philippines, 39, 74
pilot projects, 7-8, 11, 18-19, 21-22, 62, 63 (see also pioneer projects)
pioneer projects, 8, 62 (see also pilot projects)
Pirke Avot, 87
planning, 50, 91-92; comprehensive, 14, 19, 34, 83; courses in, 23-25, 26-28, 32-33; methods of, 62-64; projects, 6-8, 11, 13-14, 16-17, 18, 22-24, 26, 29-30 (see also Settlement Study Centre)
PRIDA (see Programma Integral del Desarollo Agrícola)
Programma Integral del Desarollo Agrícola (PRIDA), 23 (see also Venezuela)
project evaluation, 5, 7, 24, 75-76; problems of methodology, 61, 63-64
project identification, 5-6; problems of methodology, 61-64 (see also Division for International Cooperation)
project selection (see project identification)
Puerto Rico, 51

Rassco Construction Company, 84
Regional Asian Seminar, 49-51
regional development, 25-28 (see also regional projects; Settlement Study Centre)
regional projects, comprehensive, 28-34; Brazil, 25-28; El Sisal, 32-33; Ghazvin, 30-31; Laos, 33-34; support for, 28-29; Zambia, 31-32 (see also agricultural projects, comprehensive rural development; research institutes)

Registrar of Cooperatives, 46-47
Rehovot conferences, 34, 59-60
Rehovot Movement, 59 (see also Rehovot conferences)
Republic of the Congo, 74
research institutes, 7, 53-60 (see also CIARA; institutions; Settlement Study Centre)
research studies: agriculture, 15, 56-57; development cooperation, 91; El Sisal, 32-33; modernization, 15-16, Petrolandia, 20; scientific, 57; supervised credit, 21; youth, 38-39, 90 (see also research institutes; Settlement Study Centre)
Role of Water in Development Planning, The, 84
rural center, 13, 14; in projects, 23, 29, 31, 32-33
rural comprehensive development project (see agricultural projects, comprehensive rural development)
rural institutions, 13, 18, 21-25
rural projects (see agricultural projects)
rural sector, 10, 11, 28, 29, 34, 48, 72; doctors in, 59; in Israel, 12-15; trade unionism, 50; youth in, 38-39, 41 (see also agricultural development; agricultural projects; cooperatives; rural institutions; Settlement Study Centre; urban sector)
Rwanda, 65

scientific programs, 12, 53-54, 57-60; symposia, 55-57 (see also education; training)
Second Aliya (see immigration)
seed production, 15, 19-20, 33
settlements, agricultural, 37, 46, 47; in Israel, 10, 12, 13, 14, 15; in projects, 24, 25, 26, 31-33; women in, 42; youth movements, 37, 38 (see also collectives; communes;

131

tives; industry; planning; rural sector; Settlement Study Centre)

Venezuela, 19, 21-25, 51, 55, 63, 82, 84; Ministry for Public Works, 23, 24; Ministry of Agriculture, 23; Ministry of Health, 23
Vientiane Plains, Laos, 33
villages, 12, 13, 14, 23, 24, 28, 29, 32, 39, 40, 67, 91; cooperative, 32, 33; modernization of, 15-16, 16-17, 26 (see also collectives; communes; cooperatives; kibbutz; moshav; settlements)

water: irrigation, 15, 33-34; projects, 28, 30-31, 55-56, 80 (see also TAHAL; WRD)
Water Planning for Israel (see TAHAL)
Water Resources Development (WRD), 80, 81-82
Weizmann Institute of Science, 60
WHO (see World Health Organization)
women: in Jewish national movement, 42-43; in population, 42; role in development, 43, 44, 65-66; professional, 45, 46 (see also education, of women; MCTC;

training, of women)
Women's Section of the Trade Unions, 42
Workers Association, 48 (see also Histadrut)
Workers' Bank of Israel, 51
Workers' Banks, Latin America, 51-52
Workers Brigade, 47
World Bank, 18, 62
World Health Organization (WHO), 58
World Meteorological Organization, 70
WRD (see Water Resources Development)

youth, 11, 36, 90, education, 11, 36-41, 54; movements, 36-41, 92; programs, 11, 19, 36-41, 44, 48, 64, 73 (see also Youth Aliya)
Youth Aliya, 37-38, 41 (see also youth)

Zaïre, 45
Zambia, 31-32, 45, 65, 69, 84
ZIM, 80, 85
Zionism, 2, 10, 13, 48
Zionist-Socialist movement, 46-47

SHIMEON AMIR is assistant director-general of the Ministry for Foregin Affairs in Israel, in charge of international cooperation and economic affairs. He also serves as a part-time senior lecturer in the Department of Developing Countries of the Faculty of Social Sciences at the University of Tel Aviv.

Dr. Amir has been working at the Ministry for Foreign Affairs since 1949. He served abroad in Latin America and in Portugal, and for the last 12 years in Israel he has specialized in economic and development issues of Latin America, Asia, and Africa. He traveled widely in Latin America, Asia, and Africa, visiting and negotiating development projects with Israel participation and attending international meetings, including regional economic conferences.

For several years he wrote the editorials on international affairs in a leading weekly. He contributed articles and reviews on economic and development affairs to professional publications including *International Development Review* and *Vienna Development Institute*.

Dr. Amir holds an M.A. from the Hebrew University in Jerusalem and a Ph.D from the Autonomous National University of Mexico.

CRISIS DECISION-MAKING: *Israel's Experience in 1967 and 1973*
                    Abraham R. Wagner

ISRAEL AND IRAN: *Bilateral Relationship and Effect on the Indian Ocean Basin*
                    Robert B. Reppa, Sr.

POLITICAL PARTIES IN ISRAEL
                    David M. Zohar

THE ROLE OF COMMUNICATIONS IN THE MIDDLE EAST CONFLICT: *Ideological and Religious Aspects*
                    Yonah Alexander

URBANIZATION AND THE DEVELOPING COUNTRIES: *Report on the Sixth Rehovot Conference*
                    edited by Raanan Weitz

Date Due

Demco 38-297